Race You to the Fountain of Youth

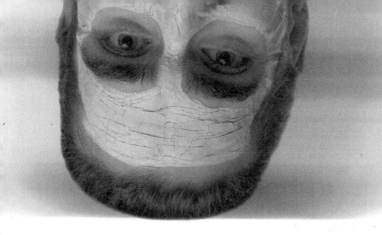

Race You to the Fountain of Youth

I'm Not Dead Yet (But parts of me are going fast)
Laughing Your Way through Midlife

Martha Bolton • Brad Dickson

Comedy Writers for Bob Hope and Jay Leno

HOWARD BOOKS
A DIVISION OF SIMON & SCHUSTER
New York   London   Toronto   Sydney

Published by Howard Books, a division of Simon & Schuster, Inc.
1230 Avenue of the Americas, New York, NY 10020

www.howardpublishing.com

Race You to the Fountain of Youth © 2007 by Martha Bolton and Brad Dickson.

Library of Congress Cataloging-in-Publication Data

ISBN-13: 978-1-4165-4399-2
ISBN-10: 1-4165-4399-6
ISBN-13: 978-1-58229-658-6 (gift edition)
ISBN-10: 1-58229-658-8 (gift edition)

10   9   8   7   6   5   4   3   2   1

HOWARD colophon is a registered trademark of Simon & Schuster, Inc.

Manufactured in the United States

For information regarding special discounts for bulk purchases,
please contact: Simon & Schuster Special Sales at 1-800-456-6798
or business@simonandschuster.com

Edited by Between the Lines
Cover design by John Lucas
Cover images: Male image © Patrick Kociniak/Design Pics/Corbis
                Female image © Big Cheese Photo LLC/Almay
Interior design by John Mark Luke Designs

To all the **plastic** surgeons, **supplement** dealers, **human growth hormone** salesmen, **aerobics** instructors, **jowl lift** specialists, and **hair plug** experts who inspired us to embark upon this race in the first place.

Contents

Contents

Contents

Contents

Acknowledgments

We would like to thank:

Denny Boultinghouse for blowing the whistle to get this race started.

Philis Boultinghouse for keeping us focused on the goal.

Dawn at Between the Lines Editorial Services for making sure we ran the race fairly and with good grammar.

Our friends and family for cheering us on each step of the way.

And, finally, Ben and Jerry's, who provided the nutrition and incentive to "hang in there" all the way to the finish line.

Ready, Set, Groan

Ladies and gentlemen, on your mark! Get set, all you middle-aged men and women, because we're all in this race together (and let's not discuss who is or is not lost).

But before we begin, there's something you should know. Men and women approach the subject of aging differently. Our attitudes are worlds apart. Our middle-age behavior, coping skills, and medical complaints are dissimilar. That's why we, the authors, decided to write this book. Men and women need to have their aging needs addressed independent of each other. It's time to celebrate our aging differences. Or better yet, whine about them.

The race to the Fountain of Youth isn't always fair. Just as one side pulls ahead, the other side might see a TV infomercial about some "miracle" vitamin concoction and gain an edge, only to lose it when the other side attends a Botox party. And on and on it goes.

Let's look at some of the diverse strategies men and women adopt as each of us approach and pass through middle age.

the **Woman's Strategy**	the **Man's Strategy**
Buys $150.00 jar of antiwrinkle facial cream	Buys $150,000 red Ferrari
Insists she doesn't need glasses	Insists he doesn't need a hearing aid
Buys exercise equipment she never uses	Joins a health club he never goes to
Covers age spots	Plucks ear hairs
Buys hip new wardrobe	Wears his once-hip clothes from the 1970s
Colors gray hairs	Suntans bald spot
Gets a derma-peel	Peels out on new Harley
Follows the new diet she just saw on *Oprah*	Orders the new menu item he just saw at the Dairy Queen
Prices a face-lift	Prices hair plugs
Gets depressed and hides in a corner of the house	Cashes out retirement fund and flies to Rio de Janeiro
Marks AARP advertisements "Return to sender"	Gladly accepts senior discounts
Refuses accurate number of candles on birthday cake	Adds even more birthday candles to warm up house and save on gas bill

Since men and women are so wonderfully unique, we felt each gender deserved its own team. Besides, the compatibility of the above strategies is tenuous on a good day.

So thank you for joining us on this race. We hope you'll enjoy the mile-by-mile, grumble-by-grumble, stumble-by-stumble, laugh-by-laugh commentary. And when all is said and done, may the better sex win.

the **Female Team**

by **Martha Bolton**

The way I see it, ladies, this race to the Fountain of Youth is ours to win. Our team is more experienced, more determined, and better funded than the men's team. Ponce de León, a man, thought he'd found the Fountain of Youth in St. Augustine, Florida. But if he did find eternal health and vitality, where is he today?

Exactly.

The last time I checked, his fountain is a tourist attraction. Nothing more. Other men have tried similar expeditions to various import car lots and hair restoration clinics, searching for the

Fountain of Youth. But these, too, were only side trips on this tantalizing journey in quest of the legendary fountain.

But most of us women believe that the Fountain of Youth can't be found by using MapQuest. Why? Because it's not a place. It's an attitude—one that can exist within each of us—that has power to keep us young. The secret of youthfulness is in a positive outlook, self-confidence, adaptability to change, the pursuit of our dreams, and a really good night cream.

But we could be wrong. And since women have never liked backing down from a challenge, we'll enter this race. After all, if there really is a Fountain of Youth, we have to be the first there to claim it for our side! So, ladies, on your mark . . .

Get set . . .

Let's go!

. . . right after my nap.

Physical Changes of the Over-Forty Woman

I Am Woman, Where'd I Go?

What over-forty woman hasn't stood in front of a mirror and succumbed to the temptation of rolling up her forehead and tucking it under her bangs to take off a few years? If we're honest, we would all admit to doing this. Why do you think big hair is coming back in style? It's to give us someplace to tape back a few of those birthdays. (I wouldn't recommend using duct tape, however. The silver tends to show through your bangs.)

Another thing we'd probably admit to, if we're honest, is watching some of those makeover shows and wondering what it would be like to actually undergo plastic surgery. Does it hurt? Can I afford it? How long is the recovery? And will they still let me in AARP if I look too young?

Some of us don't stop there. We figure, well, if I'm going under for a face-lift, why not get a different nose while I'm at it? Or a straighter smile, or higher cheekbones, or a more pronounced chin. Perhaps we'd like to add a dimple or two or get our ears stitched back or have a little liposuction on our thighs. Or maybe we'd like to hem that "chin skirt" we've started growing since we turned fifty.

I'm not ready for any of that. Not yet, anyway. The main thing holding me back is the fact that plastic surgery is still an invasive procedure. If it was something that could be done, say, in a drive-through lane and I could get on with my day, then I might be more interested. But plastic surgery is a far more complicated order than what can be handled in a drive-through. It's going to require getting out of the lane and pulling over to the side and waiting, at least until the anesthetic wears off. So I'll pass for now and leave the makeovers to braver souls. A few of them are doing enough to make up for the rest of us anyway. They're single-handedly keeping the nation's plastic surgeons in caviar.

Do you know that statistically more women get plastic surgery than men? The divide between us is shrinking, but women still win this race hands (and whatever else is heading southward) down. Maybe one reason we get more plastic surgery is that we spend a lot more time in front of the mirror than men do. And not just any mirror. We bought into the "need" to have magnifying mirrors. What were we thinking? Sure, it helps when we're trying to pluck our eyebrows, but a wrinkle magnified thirty times can be scarier than a Stephen King novel! Men know better than to buy magnifying mirrors. They may allow their barber to use one when it's time for a haircut and he needs help finding what to cut, but a man would never shave with a magnifying mirror. Instinctively he knows it's not a wise thing to do.

I've watched the makeover shows on television. The end results are usually pretty dramatic, but again, it's the process that holds me back. I think I could make it as far as getting the lines drawn on my face. That much I could handle with a minimum of anesthesia. It would be sort of like looking at model homes and imagining where your furniture would go but never actually purchasing the house. Or like taking a three-sizes-ago dress out of your closet and holding it up to your current body. You know you're not going to actually get into the dress (not without the Jaws of Life), but you can dream.

So I dream. That's all. Dream about the possibilities. It's safe and painless. Dreaming doesn't involve stitches. Besides, without a magnifying mirror, I'm content to live in my new "loosened-up" skin. It's comfortable, like an old pair of jeans that has just the right give. It's still me in there. And like women everywhere, I've earned each and every laugh and worry line.

Besides, where does all this making over stop? I watched a show recently about how teenage girls are choosing to have plastic surgery. Not because they were severely injured in an automobile accident or born with some facial disfigurement. They believe they have to have the perfect nose, the perfect smile, the perfect whatever.

But are we losing something with all this "perfection"?

When I was in school, some of the nicest people on campus

weren't the ones with the flawless facial features and perfectly chiseled physiques. They were the average- or even less-than-average-looking kids who had accepted themselves with all their less-than-perfect aspects—and accepted others with their less-than-perfect aspects, too. So maybe stopping at the presurgery lines drawn on my face isn't a bad thing to do—at least for me, at least for now. Like I said, if they ever make plastic surgery something I can get in a drive-through lane, I might reconsider. But only if I can have fries with that.

Corn Pads Are Just Another Way of Saying Happy Birthday

Corn pads, feet pillows, whatever you care to call them, one thing's for certain: For years they have not received the respect they deserve. Ever since corn pads first hit the market, most fashion circles have shunned them as inferior accessories. They don't even get mentioned in the major design showcases, even though you know with all that walking down runways, models have to be wearing them.

I say it's high time for all that to change and for corn pads to start getting some long-overdue admiration. For decades these little foot cushions have been protecting our feet and helping them heal. They do bring a different look to a dressy sandal, but all in all, corn pads are nothing to be looked down upon. (Okay, maybe we can't help but look down on them because they're on our feet, but go with me on this.)

Besides, pillows are in vogue right now. One glance at the latest sofa brochure and you can see that. The more pillows the better. And historically pillows have indicated wealth. Royalty always had plenty of pillows around to lie on while they munched on grapes and turkey legs. That being the case, there's no telling how many corn pads King Henry VIII might have worn. The high heels men wore in those days had to have given them foot problems, so if they slapped on a foot pillow or two, where was the shame in that?

That being said, there are certain things one should never do with a corn pad. It's just a respect issue. Here are a few corn-pad taboos:

- Corn pads are not Post-it notes. Do not write memos to yourself on them.

- Large corn pads should never be used as oven mitts. They stick to the pans and don't provide enough padding to insulate against intense heat.

- Corn pads were never intended to be used instead of Scotch tape in the wrapping of a gift.

- Do not use corn pads to hem your skirt or pants. It isn't really cost effective, and it won't last through more than two washings.

- Corn pads are not Band-Aids. It's overkill to wrap them around a hangnail.

- A corn pad should never be used as electrical tape. Exposing a corn pad to this type of fire hazard is considered corn-pad abuse in nine states.

If you follow the above tips, you and your corn pads should live a long and happy life together. Again, it's all about respect. And when all is said and done, isn't that what we women really want?

I'm Not Dead Yet (But Parts of Me Are Fading Fast)

Have you ever gotten out of bed in the morning and realized that only a portion of you was awake? It's like your eyes opened at eight o'clock, but the rest of you has its snooze alarm set for a half hour later. You try to get out of bed, but every movement makes you feel like you're Gumby.

I don't know about other women, but this happens to me every morning. I don't think it's a circulatory problem as much as it's a stubbornness problem. I want to get up, but my legs stubbornly insist on staying in bed. It's the same willfulness with which they keep walking over to buffet counters after my brain knows I'm full, or walking me back to my car every time I try to sign up at a gym. My legs seem to have a mind of their own.

Other body parts of mine seem to have gotten a mind of their own over the years, too. Here's the short list:

the **Female Team**

my **Body Part**	its **Misbehaviors**
Forehead	Dropping faster than the stock market after an interest-rate hike
Toenails	Growing faster than ivy (and requiring the same garden shears)
Eyes	Having more problems focusing than a roomful of ADHD students
Hair	Sadly, the thinnest part of me
Chest	What was up must come down
Stomach	I don't remember putting on a fanny pack
Curves	Then:) (Now: ( ) Enough said
Hips	Spreading faster than bird flu
Thighs	More pockets than a pair of cargo pants
Mind	If found, call owner at 1-800-555-3724

The Botox Chronicles

A new home-party opportunity is making the rounds these days. I'm not talking about food storage systems or crystal or even home decorating. I'm talking about Botox. It's a get-together with your friends and a doctor (who says doctors don't make house calls these days?) where those interested can have the procedure done and surprise their husbands with more than a lettuce crisper. It sounds a little scary to me, though. I would never consider going to my neighbor's house and having brain surgery over tea. So what's the appeal of these home Botox parties? Who knows? But I have to admit, if the parties were for one of these next procedures, I might be tempted to throw one myself.

The Underarm Lift

Considering the danger some underarms pose under a wind advisory, this procedure might entitle you to a discount on your insurance policy. It has been estimated that half of the injuries in most hurricanes are the result of severe underarm self-whippings. These can also take place under ceiling fans carelessly adjusted to the highest setting. The underarm lift could be life-saving!

The Knee Pull

My knees look like two cascade valances draped at the mid-point of my legs. Sure, it's a good place to tuck my identification when I'm at the beach, but the extra flesh can get in the way in other situations, like swimming. I keep thinking a stingray is gliding by when really it's just my knee skin floating to the surface. True, all this excess skin does give a little extra cushion when you're down on your knees washing the floor. But at this age, how often do we physically get down on our knees? Probably not very often, because we know that more often than not, it's a one-way trip.

The Heel Peel

Women frequently get facial peels, but if you really want to defy your age, the heel peel is for you. Nothing shows the wear and tear of life more than our heels. Dry, cracked, rough heels can have us snagging and dragging seaweed down the beach behind us, or scratch our hardwood floors so badly that they have to be sanded down and restained. (Helpful hint: if you can buy a sander, you can save a lot of money between regular heel peels.)

Big Toenail Reduction

It's a known fact that the older we get, the longer our toenails tend to grow. They can grow to unimaginable lengths (remember Howard Hughes?) and can take on all sorts of interesting shapes (remember Howard Hughes?). Big-toenail-reduction surgery will help you return to those happy days of yesteryear when your feet didn't look like two deluxe Swiss army knives. You'll be able to wear open-toed shoes again (we're talking shoes that were originally intended to be open-toed, not ones where your toenails simply broke through the front).

Tummy Relocation

Not to be confused with the traditional tummy tuck, the tummy relocation is a procedure whereby a surgeon relocates your stomach to another, more suitable area. It's sort of like moving to a house in the suburbs after you've outgrown the downtown condo. After relocating your stomach to a roomier area, you won't notice the extra pounds nearly as much. For instance, if those surplus ten pounds were hanging off your shoulders instead, you could pass them off as shoulder pads and join a women's football team.

We all have old photos of us with our stomachs in the place God intended them to be. But over the years, many of us have seen our stomachs slide a bit southward. And not just for the winter, either. The tummy tuck reduces the amount of fat that has deposited itself in the stomach area, but the tummy relocation is about moving it, rather than getting rid of it. With stomachs, just as with real estate, it's all about location, location, location.

Under-Chin Enhancement

If we're doomed to have that baggy skin under our chin, why not do something creative with it? In this surgery, the loose skin is either tied and stitched into a nice bow or folded over for a turtleneck look. For those not on a tight budget, pearls and other precious jewels may be added to create a permanent choker and dress it up for more formal occasions.

Chin Separation

Similar to the surgery that separates conjoined twins, the chin separation procedure divides chins that have hung out together for so long the flesh has adhered to itself. Chins have a right to coexist—closely but separately—and this surgery is helping chins all over the world achieve their rightful independence.

Earlobe Tuck

Anyone who has worn heavy earrings for more than twenty years understands the desperate need for this procedure. In an earlobe tuck, the lower portion of the ear—which now hangs like raw pizza dough waiting to be tossed into the air—is rolled under, forming a sort of croissant or cannoli, if you will. This not only keeps the earlobes off the shoulders and out of bowls of soup when the patient is eating, but can also take years off a woman's appearance.

Physical Changes of the Over-Forty Woman

The Nostril Fence

You know you're a candidate for the nostril fence when your grandkids start trying to run their Matchbox cars through your nasal passages. Unfortunately, in our later years, nostrils begin to grow for no reason at all—and won't stop until they're big enough to be listed in the Caverns of North America Guide Book. We're not sure why this is. It could be to balance out the sudden and rapid ear growth in men, but this hasn't been proven. The nostril fence works somewhat like the proposed U.S.-Mexico border fence. It partitions off much of the entry so as not to let just anything and everything pass through. In more severe cases, a border patrol guard can be added to the procedure, for an additional charge, to stay on twenty-four-hour security watch.

The Eyebrow Mow

This is an intense electrolysis procedure, so it requires sedation and a hospital stay. If you're over forty and have eyebrows so bushy they could hold up their own set of Christmas lights, the eyebrow mow is just the solution you're looking for. I'm not sure why some women hit forty and suddenly start growing a forest above their eyes while others, like me, hit middle age and start losing hair from every follicle that ever even thought about being part of an eyebrow . . . but it happens. An eyebrow maintenance agreement is available on a weekly or biweekly service basis.

The Elbow-Skin Staple

Like the knee, elbows tend to gather extra flesh during the second half of life. The medical term for this condition is *elbow-sagation,* and while not fatal, it's not a welcomed part of middle age. The extra skin can easily get caught in our purse clasps or in doors, and sometimes it can even get tangled up in our steering wheel while we're driving and cause a serious accident or continuous honking.

Things We Did Back Then That We're Paying for Now

Some of us did things in our youth without ever considering the consequences of our actions. Some of these consequences wouldn't be realized for years to come. But payday's here. Below are just a few of our misguided attitudes and the result many of us are having to face now:

Item or Situation	Attitude Then	Attitude Now
Sunburn	Sunblock? Are you kidding?	I wonder if I can use Nu-Vinyl on my face.
Hair spray	I love my beehive!	Didn't we used to have an ozone layer?
Credit cards	Buy now, pay later. How fun is this?!	Original bill for eight-track tape player: $42. Paid over a thirty-three-year period: $4,698. Finally cutting up credit cards into a million little pieces and sending them back to the company: priceless.
Rock concerts	Groovy! Can you dig it?	Eh? What's that? Can you speak up?
Slept through English class	What's the big deal?	It dedn't hert mi eny.
Steady diet of pizza, hot dogs, and double cheeseburgers	My metabolism works it off faster than I can eat it.	My metabolism didn't just slow down. It pulled over and parked.
Ignoring that annoying brainy kid who was always bugging you in class	What a nerd!	I wonder what ever happened to little Billy Gates?

Is It Really Possible?

Plenty of women have passed the Great Age Divide (the other side of forty) and have come through looking just as good as, if not better than, they did in their younger years. People like Suzanne Somers, Diane Keaton, and Sophia Loren would be considered beautiful, fit, and youthful. The fact that they're boomers makes their appearance and attitude even more impressive.

In interviews Sophia Loren has said that one of her secrets to looking and feeling young is eating pasta and bathing in virgin olive oil. See, that's where I went wrong. For years I thought she had said the secret was bathing in pasta. No wonder my skin hasn't improved any and always feels a little starchy.

Another secret often cited by youthful boomers is a good attitude and a love of life. It's hard to be a grouch and look young. Let's consider some of the well-known grouches in literature.

- *The Grinch*—wrinkled, greenish complexion, a permanent sneer, untrimmed fingernails the length of a bass boat. Does he say youth and vitality to you?

- ***Scrooge***—bent over, unkempt hair, always complaining and barking out orders, friendless. Think about it. Could he be the poster boy for the Fountain of Youth?

Grumpiness is the enemy of youthfulness. It can age us faster than California smog. So instead of worrying about whether our faces need a lift, perhaps we should try giving our attitudes a lift instead. We just might be surprised at how many years it takes off our appearance. But if we do that and still have a Grinch-green complexion, maybe it's time to start cutting back on those meat-loaf specials on the Over Fifty menu.

All in How You Look at It

A Woman's Advantages in Living to One Hundred

- By then, you will have hit every outlet mall in the galaxy.

- You will have outlived every person who ever got on your nerves.

- You'll get to scoff at everyone who ever told you that a steady diet of cheesecake would shorten your life.

- That fifty-dollar dress you charged on MasterCard back in 1993 will finally be paid off.

- Chances are good that you might get asked on a date by Ashton Kutcher.

- Your high school cheerleading uniform will be accepted by the Smithsonian.

- You can use your birthday candles to cook with and save a bundle on your gas bill.

- Your number will finally be called at the DMV.

- The butterfly you got tattooed on your shoulder back in the seventies will have slid down to your ankle. Two tattoos for the price of one.

Fifty Cents and Two Box Tops

Do you remember all those cereal-box offers they used to have when we were growing up? You'd hardly see a cereal box that didn't offer us something. Maybe you remember sending away for a few of these yourself:

- Shirley Temple cereal bowl and pitcher

- Tony the Tiger spoon

- Miniature table tennis set

- Junior fire marshal ring

- Tigereye marble

- Lucky Charms leprechaun

- Post Toasties Indian headdress

Most of these trinkets arrived in the mail a few weeks after we requested them. Some may still be en route. They did make childhood fun, though, didn't they?

Remember when gas stations gave away free drinking glasses or dishes with a fill-up? They also gave away stamps—either blue chip or green stamps—and you could save books and books of them to redeem for some pretty nice household items. It's how many of us furnished our homes when we first got married. Nowadays the most we can expect from some gas stations is a week-old hot dog and an out-of-order restroom.

By marriage I am now part owner in one inch of land in the Canadian Yukon, thanks to another premium offer. The inches of land were sold through a special offer by the Quaker Oats company, and my husband, a youngster at the time, had the foresight to get in on the deal. Donald Trump would be proud. The television tie-in was Sergeant Preston of the Yukon. As you'll no doubt recall, Sergeant Preston was a member of the Canadian Royal Mounties. With his dog, Yukon King, and his horse, Rex, this police officer solved crimes, helped the downtrodden, and apparently captured the imaginations of young land developers the world over with the possibility of actually owning a piece of Canadian real estate.

I'm not sure how many labels my husband had to send in or how much money he had to save up (he believes it was a dollar), but he does recall that they sent him an actual land deed. We haven't tried to sell his holdings yet, or even get a loan on the inch "ranch," but we might look into that someday. It's probably not a big enough plot to build a cabin on, but we might be able to use it for vacation property and go hunting or fishing on it. We could fish for sardines.

Since no investor meetings have been held over the years,

something tells me that those in charge figured folks would forget all about owning their inch of land, and the property would remain with the company or promotional agency. We've thought about finding other inch owners and forming an Inch Owners Organization so we'd have some say in how our inches are being developed. But it's probably too cold up there to stage a protest march. I guess it's like those stars you can have named after you . . . for a price. It's a nice thought, but how would you check on it?

Someday you may be able to take a rocket there and put up a sign that says "Welcome to Betty's Star, stop and sit a spell," but in the meantime you'll have to take the company's word that it's your star—much as my husband has had to do with his inch of Yukon. Then again, that could be one of the secrets to our lasting marriage. We wouldn't want to go through a nasty property-division battle. After all, if your building choices are limited with one inch of land, they're even slimmer on a half inch of land.

I do miss those good old days of the mail-in premiums and gas-station giveaways, especially with the high cost of housing these days. Who wouldn't rather eat a truckload of Quaker Oats and buy a piece of land an inch at a time than to have to qualify for an interest-only, balloon payment due in three years type of loan. But life's not that easy.

You can, though, still get a pretty good toy inside a child's meal at fast-food restaurants . . . if you're not above wearing a crown and drinking your beverage out of a kiddie cup.

Can't Take It With You

I'm in the middle of cleaning up some of my clutter, trying to downsize so my stacks of paper can fit into a room smaller than the Smithsonian, and I've got to say, I've even been surprising myself over some of the things I've held on to all these years. If you've ever helped anyone over the age of forty move, or if you've been part of an estate sale, you know I'm not alone in this.

When it comes to our possessions, it's hard to know what to save and what to get rid of. Web auction sites like eBay haven't helped matters, either. They've got us looking at our old junk with new eyes. We're pulling our worn-out 1980s reindeer slippers from the back of the closet and wondering at what price we should start the bidding.

Antiques Roadshow stories of rare finds only add to this behavior. If some man from Albuquerque can pick up an old painting at a flea market, take it out of its frame, and discover a missing van Gogh underneath, how in the world are we going to part with our Elvis on velvet?

Even scraps of paper could be important. I've gone through boxes and boxes of papers only to find a dollar bill tucked away in the middle: proof positive that it was worth the fourteen years (and a spider bite) it took me to go through that stack!

the **Female Team**

The problem most women face is what will happen to our prized possessions after our passing. We have to come to terms with the fact that our loved ones are probably not going to waste time going through all of our souvenirs and memorabilia. Everything we "couldn't live without" is going to be out on the curb faster than they can say, "May she rest in peace." Oh, they might save things easily identified as having some value. The loose change, the savings account, the inch-of-land deed. But if it's something that requires a little research to determine its worth, chances are the whole lot of it will be gone with the wind and the sanitation truck on the next trash day.

So why aren't more of us going through it ourselves and separating what's truly of value from what's just junk cluttering up our lives? Good question. The answer might be that we're stuck. By hanging on to this stuff, do we think we're preserving a part of the youthful us? Are we keeping that dress we wore for our junior high graduation so we can conjure up that junior high image of us when we're feeling a little down? Is it the same with that sweatshirt from our college days? Or our wedding gown or our children's baby outfits?

Much of what I've kept over the years has some kind of emotional significance. Not only do I have every piece of art my kids ever made for me, but I've got some of the art I made for my own parents! I have keys from our last four houses, magazines from the 1980s (no emotional attachment to these, just guilt for having bought them and never read them), and T-shirts that haven't fit me since the Cheesecake Factory first opened its doors. I'm not a pack rat. I just want to go through it all before I toss it out, and I just haven't had the time. For years. There's enough paper stacked in my office to account for the disappearance of at least three forests. And the paper trail doesn't end there. It oozes on down the hallway and into a few other rooms of the house as well. Rolled up, I'd have enough paper fire logs to last through another ice age.

One of the reasons that I can't seem to throw away paper is that most of it has my writing notes scribbled on it. These can be hard to read twelve years later. In fact, some of them appear to have been written in a different language. It's going to take years to sort through all these notes and find an interpreter. But I'll do it. Eventually.

Another thing I tend to hoard is old receipts. I'm afraid to throw anything like that away. If I ever get audited for the 1969 tax year, I'm ready.

I also keep souvenirs from places I've visited. I've got souvenir matchboxes from restaurants that have long since gone out of business (probably because they gave away too many matchboxes).

So why do we do it? Why do we hang on to all this stuff? All of these things we think we can't possibly do without, until we see the same thing offered on an Internet auction site for a couple hundred bucks, and suddenly we discover just how easily we can let it go and list it for sale.

I believe one of the reasons is that our piles represent our lives. They're our personal history. We've lived. We've been here. And we have proof. They can take everything else from us, but they can't have our beta recorder. Or our computer that crashed back in '89 (we're going to get it fixed any day now), or our broken treadmill (it jammed when the pillow got stuck in the conveyor belt in '92). These are our things! Part of our identity is tied up in them. They satisfy our need for validation, and it's this need that keeps us hauling all our stuff from apartment to apartment, house to house, and eventually retirement home to retirement home. It's our way of saying to the world, and to the garbage man, "It's all mine, and no landfill on earth is going to get it!" (Or, for some of us, "No landfill on earth could hold it all!")

Then again, we haven't yet seen what we could get for it all on eBay.

Video Farewells

One of the newest ways to say good-bye to a loved one is with a "video tombstone." Instead of the regular grave marker that simply lists the deceased's name, span of life, and a nice sentiment, the video tombstone takes the memory marker concept even further. Visitors can press a button and be shown a brief video biography of the dearly departed.

Imagine it: soon a stroll through a graveyard will be like strolling through the documentary section at Blockbuster. No longer will you have to wonder about the lives of the people whose graves you're passing. Now you'll be able to learn a little something about them without disturbing them in the least. Actually, it's a pretty nice way to honor someone's life.

One problem I can see with the video tombstone, however, is the potential for commercial marketing. Given the current trend of advertisers bombarding us at every possible opportunity, companies are likely to start pressuring memorial parks to allow them to advertise on the video tombstones. Aside from the obvious respect issues, I don't think selling advertising time on grave markers is a good idea. I don't know about you, but walking through a cemetery and hearing, "Head On! Apply directly to the forehead. Head On! Apply directly to the forehead!" could be even more irritating than it is now.

Another potential problem could be with the video itself. How you're remembered in life might depend on how your video biography turns out. What if all your husband, children, or extended family can afford is the low-budget package? You may be fine with that . . . until the grave next to you goes to some woman whose family hires Ron Howard to produce hers. Or worse yet, what if your estranged stepdaughter volunteers to do the video? You could end up looking like Attila the Hun with no way to defend yourself.

One way to protect against this is to produce your own video ahead of time. That way you can make sure the important highlights of your life are covered, the motives behind each of your decisions are clear and not left to interpretation, and the background music you like is played. There's nothing worse than having to spend eternity listening to music you hated while you were alive. (Again, the stepdaughter.) It does make sense, though, that since you're the only one who knows the whole story of your life, you should be the one to make these end-of-life decisions.

Having your memorial written ahead of time is nothing new. News organizations write these in advance all the time. If a celebrity is suddenly rushed to the hospital or is engaging in risky behavior, like signing up for sky-surfing lessons, the news director will assign someone to write an obituary so the station won't be caught off guard should the star die. The eulogy will be ready to go while the celebrity is still very much alive and only her career is dead. So writing up your own obituary before you're dead is perfectly acceptable.

Have you ever thought about what you would want covered in a summary of your life? What have been some of the highlights so far of your time here on earth? What accomplishments or actions make you most proud? What legacy do you hope to leave to your children and grandchildren? Who has been the biggest influence on your life? What's your favorite color, your favorite flower, your favorite song? What's the most important thing in your life? What do you believe? What wisdom have you gained? What lessons have you learned? What fears have you conquered? What life truths would you like to leave with your family so they can benefit from your experiences and have a little easier go of it? What has been your life's message? And most important, do you think your husband, children, siblings, parents, and other family members and close friends know your answers to these questions?

If not, you might want to buy one of those blank books and write some of these things down. You might also start asking those around you how they would describe your life, your values, and your passions. You might be surprised to hear, perhaps even for the first time, of the positive impact you've made on someone's life. So surprised that it might cause you to refocus and rewrite the second half of your biography, this time concentrating on what's really important and minimizing what isn't.

A Few Minor Adjustments

Driving Tips

I'm proud to say that my mother scored 100 percent on the last driving test she took before she passed away. I was so proud of her at the time that I made copies of her test and handed them out to family members (having quilts made from it would have taken too long).

I don't know if I could get 100 percent on my driving test today, and I'm nearly twenty years younger than she was when she aced hers. It just goes to show that age has little to do with whether you're a good driver. Mom knew the rules of the road and preferred driving in the slow lane of the freeway no matter how far she had to go.

She had good reflexes. She braked faster than anyone I know, regardless of whether there was a reason for it. This was back before seat belts were mandatory, so to be able to stop on a dime and not send your passengers through the windshield took skill and experience—and a strong right arm that she threw in front of you with enough force to knock the wind out of you. This maneuver is known as the "mom restraint."

the **Female Team**

Still, since some of us could benefit from a refresher course, here are some driving tips for the middle-aged female driver:

- When using the rearview mirror to apply lipstick, be sure to allow the distance of at least one car length per ten miles of speed between you and the driver in front of you. For example, if you're driving at a speed of seventy miles per hour, you would want to keep seven car lengths between you and the next vehicle. If you're applying mascara as well, increase the distance by half a car's length. Per eye.

- To avoid swollen ankles on long road trips, stretch your legs at regular intervals. If your car has cruise control, I recommend the full leg stretch. Set the cruise control to the speed limit, then place both legs up on the dashboard and stretch. If your car doesn't have cruise control, do only one leg at a time.

- Contrary to what some older women believe, the car will operate without the turn signal on. After executing your turn, you may turn it off. It's no longer necessary to drive with the signal on for the entire length of the state.

- Just for clarification—the N on the gear shift stands for "neutral," not "napping."

- Some tires lose traction when driven through water. Stay out of lakes. It could just be a MapQuest misprint.

- Air-bag deployment is for safety purposes only. If you really feel you need a pillow to drive, bring one from home.

- Driving with the emergency brake on is hard on your brakes. Never do it if the flames from the overheated brakes are leaping higher than the roof of your car. This decreases visibility and is a driving hazard. It also adds more heat to your hot flashes. Need I say more?

- Panty hose should never be changed at the same time you're changing lanes or executing a left turn. This could cause irreparable damage to the panty hose. Change panty hose only on right turns—but stop first if the light is red, then proceed.

- Only drive in the forward direction. Postal workers do this to cut down on accidents. From what I understand, it works. Keeping your car in park can help. Usually.

Frankly, I've never liked driving in reverse. I don't like the crunching sound when you back into things.

Not long ago my grown son was letting me borrow his car because it could carry more family members than mine could, and since he was going to work and everyone else was with me, I needed the larger vehicle. Now, you have to get this scene in your head. My son loves his car. It's his baby. So for him to hand me his keys was a major concession. Of course, he wouldn't let go of them until I promised to bring the car back in one piece and unharmed. I wondered how he thought I could guarantee that, but I promised anyway. I got into the car, buckled up, made sure everyone else was buckled up, then shifted to reverse and pressed down on the gas pedal. I had no compelling reason to put the car in reverse. I could just as easily have gone forward, but I wanted to emphasize the extreme care with which I was handling his car. I thought he must be impressed as he stood there watching me. That is, until our beautiful moment was interrupted by that awful crunching sound.

"What in the world . . . ?" I gasped, wondering what I could have hit, since there wasn't a thing behind me. I looked toward my son to see if he knew, but he was frozen in horror and disbelief. I had no idea his mouth could open that wide.

He had just handed me the keys. I hadn't driven more than twenty feet in reverse (again, to show how far I would back up to be safe), and already I had crashed into something!

As it turned out, that something was a light pole. (Okay, I should have seen a light pole sticking up in the middle of a parking lot; but it was painted gray, the same color as his car's interior, and well, it just blended in.)

All things considered, my son took it pretty well . . . once we resuscitated him. But like I said, keeping a car in the forward gear should cut down on this sort of seemingly "unavoidable" accident.

Temporary, Nonsurgical Procedures for the Budget-Minded Woman over Forty

Many of us simply can't afford the high cost of plastic surgery, even if we wanted it. So here are some alternative measures for the budget-minded woman over forty.

- *Duct tape.* Placed strategically, this handy miracle tape can take years off your appearance and make those cheerleaders at your high school reunion green with envy. And if your school colors included silver, all the better!

- *A one-size-too-small choker.* This necklace is the perfect accessory for tucking in any loose skin under the chin.

- *Facial mask.* Apply as directed, only never peel off. This will tighten and firm your skin. Some facial masks might give your cheeks a greenish or bluish tint, so accessorize accordingly.

- *Bangs and stray facial hairs.* When overgrown, they can hide a multitude of years.

- *Removing all mirrors from your home and car.* What you don't see, you can't lose sleep over.

- *Hanging weights on the ends of your hair.* This will pull on your roots and force your forehead skin to reverse its direction and fall backward instead of forward, easily taking off at least ten years.

- *Photoshop.* Use this computer program to touch up your family photographs. You're as young as you look in your latest photos: now you can look even better than your grandkids with the simple click of a mouse.

- *Smiling.* A broad smile can pull up sagging jowls, put a youthful twinkle in your eyes, and expose all your laugh lines. Wear them proudly!

Popular Sports Adjusted for the Woman over Forty

Skydiving

Same as regular skydiving, only the jump involves floating back up to the plane at least once midjump to make sure you didn't forget something.

Figure Skating

Not only can an over-forty woman do this as well as a woman half her age, but she can do it while carrying a purse!

Bowling

Many women over forty participate in this sport—not for the exercise—for the roomy shoes. Nothing handles puffy feet better than a good pair of bowling shoes.

Soccer

By the time a woman gets to forty years of age, she's encountered enough difficult people to give her a good selection from which to choose a face to paint on the soccer ball. Once she's narrowed it down to the final one, she can kick the likeness to her heart's content.

NASCAR

Women can drive fast, too. Even the over-forty woman. The only difference is, for the over-forty NASCAR races, drivers are required to stay in the slow lane with their left turn signal on. The winner is the first to find a Waffle House along the speedway.

Women's (Skin) Tag Football

Similar to regular tag football, with one small exception: I'm not saying what the players have to pull on to score a "tackle," but this sport has already put four thousand dermatologists out of business.

Women's Boomer Baseball

Baseball with just one small tweak in the rules: any hairpieces or loose body parts that fly off the runner and land on home plate before she gets there herself still count as a point.

Women's Boomer Basketball

Like regular basketball, only when a boomer gets called out for excessive dribbling, the ref usually calls for a mop.

Women's Boomer Skiing

Nothing is quite as beautiful as watching a boomer make her way down a snow-covered slope, twisting to the right, curving to the left, doing a perfect double flip and ultimately coming to rest at the bottom of the hill. If done on purpose, that's even better.

The Boomer-Friendly Mall

Female baby boomers love to shop. But malls keep getting bigger and bigger, and no one has come up with a way for us to enjoy the shopping experience without wearing ourselves out. And since most of us left our bowling shoes back at the bowling alley, we have to find another solution.

What we need are boomer-friendly malls. Airports have bullet trains that take us from one concourse to another. Why don't malls offer these for shoppers? We can board at, say, Macy's and get off at Sears or Penney's or some other store.

Here are some other suggestions that would help us with mall shopping:

- *Sale bins exclusively for the slower shopper.* After middle age, sometimes our reach just isn't what it used to be. Why should we have to compete with the younger and more aggressive shoppers? A separate, slower-shopper sale bin would even things out and improve our chances of scoring a good bargain.

- *Mirror-free dressing rooms.* As far as I know, the Constitution still protects us from cruel and unusual punishment. And what could be crueler than a dressing-

room mirror—or more unusual than the effect that
overhead lighting has on our faces?

- *Larger numbers on price tags.* Larger in font size, not in
  price or size number.

- *Fewer unruly children running around unattended,
  which leads to tantrums that can get out of hand.* We'd
  rather not have to throw a tantrum, but what else can we
  do when the kids won't let go of the items we want?

- *Boomer-designated parking.* Exercise is healthy, but
  having to park two counties away and walk to and from
  the mall is something we'd rather not do . . . especially
  with an armful of shopping bags.

- *A place to set our purses in the restrooms.* No telling
  where that floor has been. Also, please limit the automatic
  flushes to one per customer.

- *Nicer store clerks.* If it takes a while to locate our cash
  or credit card, be patient. Our money is good whether
  we whip it out of our purses quickly or have to send in a
  purse-diving team.

- *Better styles for our age group.* Not all of us want to go
  through life looking like Britney Spears or Paris Hilton.

We'd gladly pay a little more for another inch or two of material at the bottom of our shirts.

- ***No one stopping us as we're walking through the center of the mall and asking if we want our rings cleaned, a massage, or lotion on our hands.*** If we do, we'll stop and ask you for it. Otherwise, just let us shop. We don't mean to be rude, but many of us have a long history of people-pleasing and will end up spending money we don't have on things we don't need. Please help us help ourselves.

On a more positive note, we want to thank you for opening your doors early and allowing us to get our morning exercise by mall-walking. This is kind of you. The only thing missing is a couple of pit bulls running loose to make it seem more like the outdoors.

Getting Out the Vote

Some years ago senior citizens were accused of adversely affecting the outcome of a certain presidential election. They were blamed for not being able to read the instructions on the ballots and punching their voter cards incorrectly. I wasn't there, so I don't know what happened, but I don't think it's the fault of the senior women. If anyone is thorough, it is a senior woman. No one locks her house as many times as she does, or checks and rechecks to make sure the stove is turned off. Only a senior citizen will reach her hand into a mailbox after dropping in her monthly payments, just to make sure she had a stamp on each envelope.

If anything is wrong with our voting system, I would have to say that it's the voting machines, or perhaps some of the election volunteers, or even the ballots themselves. It cannot possibly be elderly women. Elderly women are some of this country's best and most thorough voters. They'll show up at the polls even if they have to take a taxi. They'll come with all their voter information materials literally covered in notations, proof positive that they've actually read it. Compare this to the average citizen, who reads the initiatives for the first time inside the voting booth.

Older women also have no problem with producing identification at the voting precinct. Not only do they have a driver's license with them, but they'll also bring along their birth certificate, baptismal certificate, two months' worth of utility bills, their retirement check stub, and a backstage pass for a Jan and Dean concert held in the sixties.

There's no way these gals are going to get turned away from a voting booth. That's why, during the Bush versus Gore election, I knew the reported cases of disenfranchisement among Palm Beach's elderly could not have been the women.

Even after casting their ballots, most older women will continue supervising their ballot, making sure every one of the election workers, the other citizens standing in line, and the janitor at the school where the vote is being held knows that they voted. These women's votes aren't going to slip by anyone.

In my twenties I could never understand why politicians paid so much attention to Medicare issues. Now it all makes sense. Considering the way seniors honor their right to vote, it's no wonder politicians cater to this part of our population. They know this is one voting bloc you want on your side. If one of these sweet, white-haired ladies likes you, she will defend you unconditionally—and most important, she'll show up on Election Day.

I don't think my mother ever missed an election. As soon as my parents got home from work on Election Day, they would take off for the polls. My father was a Democrat. My mother was a Republican. They usually just canceled each other out, but they believed in the honor and privilege of casting their ballots.

The older I get, the more I'm interested in the political scene, too. I'm not sure why this is, but it seems to be something that kicks in during middle age and builds in intensity as we get older. It's sort of like men wearing plaid pants and suspenders. It just starts happening at a certain age, and no one knows why.

I think it's good, though. Not the plaid pants, but voting. If middle-aged and senior women don't voice their opinions on issues that matter to them, who's going to do it? The twenty- and thirty-somethings? They're too busy with their own concerns. They're voting for initiatives like extending their student loans another forty years.

Voting is important. I don't know if it will lengthen our lives any, but it does require some physical exertion to get to the precinct, so that's healthy. Trying to figure out how to operate the new voting machine certainly gives us a mental workout. But we do it. We don't surrender our right to vote for anything or anyone. The main thing voting does for us is, when a politician really messes things up, it gives us the right to say, "Hey, don't blame me. I voted for the other guy!" Or girl, as the case may be.

If Menopausal Women
Ruled the World

Menopausal women could bring certain leadership qualities to the political table that are not found in men.

For one thing, uncontrollable sweating. Men interpret this as a sign of weakness, especially in negotiations; but the menopausal woman has learned to use profuse sweating to her advantage. She realizes that streams of sweat snaking their way down a woman's face give the other party the false impression that she is nervous and unsure of herself. This, along with a good mop, can give her the advantage.

The unpredictability of a menopausal woman is another leadership advantage. Why is it that we as Americans always find ourselves having to walk on eggshells around unpredictable and volatile foreign leaders? Why not let them worry about us for a change? When they see that we have a menopausal woman that close to the red phone, they'll know we're a force to be reckoned with.

Lastly, if menopausal women ruled the world, you could rest assured that there would *never* be a nuclear war. Why? What menopausal woman in her right mind would add more heat to the planet?

Taking Care

Dream Doctor

Unlike most men, women love going to the doctor. It's almost as good as being taken out to dinner and a movie. It's akin to an evening of uninterrupted Internet shopping. We'll not only circle the appointment date on our calendars, but we'll schedule enough preparation time to include a full leg shave. That's how important a doctor's visit is to us.

The reasons for this are varied. Women love to go to the doctor because . . .

- He has a sympathetic ear for all our complaints, no matter how trivial, in spite of the fact that he will answer four emergency cell-phone calls while we're in the examination room (two of them from the golf course).

- No one is around to rebut the statement that our elbow injury was a result of housework instead of carrying packages home from the mall.

- In many cases, we get a male's undivided attention for at least fifteen minutes, and there won't be a single sports game on a TV anywhere.

- An X-ray may be the first time all year that anyone's actually taken a picture of us.

- After listening to our heart, the doctor can affirm that even though we sometimes feel invisible in our world, we are in fact still very much alive.

- Everyone loves to be caressed, and for some of us a blood pressure cuff might be just the thing to meet that need.

- A diagnosis of even the most nonthreatening illness is usually enough to get us out of cooking dinner. The quality of restaurant we get taken to depends solely on the difficulty of pronouncing the name of the condition or medical procedure.

- We can impress the doctor with how much medical knowledge we've gained from watching *Oprah*.

- We can also impress ourselves with how many different shapes we can make out of a stack of tongue depressors.

This is by no means a complete list of the benefits a woman gets from visiting her doctor, but it will give you an idea of why we look forward to the experience and will cancel almost anything else before canceling an appointment with our physician.

I should caution you, however, that some of us will sometimes misinterpret a male doctor's professional care for something more than it is. Depending on a woman's emotional hunger, it's easy to take the words, "It looks like I'm going to have to remove your spleen," to mean, "I think I love you." This is quite common. So we have to beware of running up unnecessary medical bills just because we're enjoying the attention. Body scans will not give us the closeness we may be missing in our lives, no matter how cramped the MRI machine is.

Sometimes we can even have these feelings of transference with doctors on the Web. If our husband happens to be in the other room eating popcorn and watching the game on television, should we really be on the Net conversing with a doctor about moles? This isn't healthy. We may fool ourselves into thinking the conversation is about something more than moles, but it's not. It's about moles.

Web doctors can be convenient, though. On some of the sites you can just put in your list of symptoms, and it will tell you what ailment you're most likely suffering from. You have to be careful, though. One site told me I had a virus and could shut down at any minute. I went to three specialists before figuring out it was referring to my computer.

the **Female Team**

Another problem is that women tend to self-diagnose. If we have a pain, we think we know exactly what's causing it. We'll even diagnose the symptoms of our friends. And complete strangers. We read a magazine article or watch a couple of talk shows, and we think it's as good as a medical degree.

Here's a sample of the diseases some of us have diagnosed without the help of a single blood test or X-ray.

Symptom	Diagnosis
Pain on right side	Most probably appendicitis, gallstones, or a Republican-controlled Congress
Pain on left side	Gastroenteritis or a Democratic president
Headache	Migraine, high or low blood sugar, or an overdose of news shows
Hacking cough	Bronchitis, secondhand smoke, or a good way to get a row to yourself on an airplane
Abdominal swelling	Pregnancy, stress, or postbuffet syndrome
Swelling of lower extremity	Gout, spider bite, or too-tight spandex shorts
Fatigue	Mononucleosis or late-night Diamonique sale on QVC
Rash	Poison ivy, allergic reaction, or thighs rubbing against each other while walking
Fever	Flu, pneumonia, husband turned thermostat up to "volcano" setting again
Leg cramps	Magnesium deficiency, restless legs syndrome, getting tangled in a yoga position
Insomnia	Husband's snoring, too much stress, rock band moved in next door
Drooling	Dental work, bite from a rabid bat, commercial for Krispy Kreme Doughnuts
Sore throat	Diphtheria, tonsillitis, too much screaming at a Neil Diamond concert
Itchy scalp	Psoriasis, dandruff, hives over the new tax forms
Hoarseness	Laryngitis, repeatedly saying no to telemarketers, yelling at your bank over ATM fees

Not only do we give amateur diagnoses, but we try to one-up each other with our ailments. It doesn't matter what disease one woman may have, another woman will feel she has to outdo her.

It's almost like a card game: "I'll see your defective gallbladder and raise you one heart murmur and a kidney stone."

We may enjoy talking about our illnesses, but unlike men, we don't usually let our ailments incapacitate us. We keep right on working through a heart attack. "I'm having excruciating pain in my chest right now, my jaw is hurting, and I'm sweating more than any hot flash I've ever had. But I promised I'd get these turkey costumes down to the school by noon. Then I'll grab a bite at Taco Bell, run by the bank and the post office, and after that I'll drive over to the hospital and get it checked out. I'm sure it's nothing."

Knowing what happens to us in the presence of a doctor, you would think we'd be rushing over there. He'll tell us we're having a heart attack and all we'll hear is, "Mon cherie, your lips . . . I have never seen such a beautiful shade of blue. Kiss me!"

We'll smile, tell him we're married, and just before we slip into unconsciousness, we'll rearrange the furniture in his office and make a nice doily out of the cotton balls.

You Are What You Eat

Most women over forty really do try to watch what we eat. But it would be a lot easier if the word from the medical community were consistent. They keep changing their minds about what's good for us and what isn't. Here's just a small sampling of some of the things they've changed their minds about over the years:

Postively Bad for Us	Not So Bad for Us
Eggs	Eggs
Cranberry sauce	Cranberry sauce
Chocolate	Chocolate
Coffee	Coffee
Butter	Butter
Margarine	Margarine
Microwaved foods	Microwaved foods
Splenda	Splenda
Red food coloring	Red food coloring
Apples	Apples
Milk	Milk
Tuna	Tuna

The way they keep changing their minds, how are we supposed to keep up? And the marketing moguls don't help either. As soon as the Department of Health starts preaching against fried foods, turkey fryers start popping up in stores all across the

the **Female Team**

country. The Department of Health tells us that barbecued meats could be carcinogenic, and what happens? The international barbecue contest held in Memphis every May doubles in attendance. It's like whatever they tell us is bad for us, we eat anyway because we're banking on their changing their minds in a few years.

Maybe the real truth will turn out to be more like the following:

the **Accusation**	the **Truth**
Fried foods increase your risk of heart attack	Fried foods lubricate your veins, making it easier for the occasional blood clot to pass through unhindered
Consuming animal skin poses a serious health threat	Only if the animal is still using it
Desserts should be eaten with caution	Desserts should be eaten with coffee
Gravy is not a health food	Gravy is what you pour over health food to make it edible
Woman cannot live on chocolate alone	Nougat and caramel are necessary, too.
Dairy products can cause gallstones	This risk is greatly reduced when the cream is whipped and sitting on top of a banana split
Carrot cake doesn't count as a vegetable	Actually, it provides all four basic food groups: grain (flour), dairy (cream-cheese frosting), vegetables and fruits (carrots), and protein (eggs and nuts)
Cheesecake can cause hardening of the arteries	And your point is?
Doughnuts are not a balanced meal	They are, too. With the proper concentration, you can easily learn to balance a dozen boxes on your head
Ben & Jerry's ice cream should be eaten only in moderation	Where is the town of Moderation?
The dessert "Death by Chocolate" can cause death by chocolate	What a way to go!

How to Calculate Your Real Age

First of all, why? Sure, there's been much discussion of late about a woman's "real" age. A "real age" isn't your birthday age. It's your body's age. Using a special chart and factoring in lifestyle, health, and hereditary information, you can now calculate the "real age" of your body.

But did we ask for this? Many women have a hard enough time accepting the age our birth certificate indicates, much less the age our body's saying we are.

I don't know how accurate these kinds of tests are, anyway. I've taken a few, and it seems to me they missed some of the most obvious age-determining factors. Here are a few questions I felt were missing from these tests.

- If you use the valet parking service at the mall, especially during the holiday season, instead of driving around the complex seven or eight times trying to find an empty parking space, subtract two years from your body's age.

- If you've missed two of the last four family get-togethers, at which your mother always asks why you're still married to the same loser, subtract four years.

the **Female Team**

- If your diet plan includes carnival house mirrors that elongate and thin out your body so you never again have to think about another stupid diet, subtract five years.

- If you've blocked all news programs from your television set, subtract eight years.

- If you've added your telephone and cell-phone numbers to the Do Not Call list so telemarketers can't find you, subtract four years and six months.

- If you blew all your retirement money on a bad investment, subtract five years, because now that you're broke you'll never again have to worry about losing your retirement money.

- If you are completely debt free, subtract seven years (and send any money you don't want to us, in care of this publisher).

- If the person you voted for is in office and you're glad you voted for him or her, subtract six years.

- If the person you voted for is in office and you're sorry you voted for him or her but are currently in therapy to get over it, subtract four years.

A Woman's Guide to Living Longer

Here are eight key behavior modifications for women to follow in order to live a longer and more fulfilling life:

- Cut your stress in half: only open your mail every other day.

- Reduce your intake of fat: scoop out the filling (save it for later) before eating that box of Ding Dongs.

- Improve your outlook on life: have your windows cleaned.

- Get an annual checkup. Not only will you discover any medical condition, but you'll be revitalized by that two-hour nap in the doctor's waiting room.

- Take a multivitamin every day. Stuff it in your Twinkies.

- Drive defensively. Buy a tank on eBay.

- Give generously—and not just a piece of your mind.

- Avoid negative people. Like pool servicemen, they'll only drain you.

Times Change

We Interrupt This Program . . .

In years past, breaking news reports used to be about something of significance that had just happened in the world—a country had been attacked, a riot had broken out, an armed and dangerous escaped convict was on the loose, or Hershey's just went on sale. Now it seems our favorite programs are interrupted with "breaking news" like who's being seen with Britney, who Jessica's breaking up with, and what's the latest Hollywood feud.

Here are some breaking news announcements I'm expecting to hear any day now:

- "We interrupt tonight's Washington report to remind you that this is not your favorite daytime soap opera. This drama is for real."

- "We interrupt today's *Rugrats* to remind any moms who might be watching that these are not your home movies."

the **Female Team**

- "We interrupt our tornado-damage coverage to remind mothers of teenagers that their bedrooms could always look worse."

- "We interrupt this diet commercial to give you time to grab a snack."

- "We interrupt this reality show to clarify that worms and beetles are not suitable dinner fare, no matter how angry you are with your husband."

- "We interrupt this home-remodeling show because the men featured are too handy around the house and could evoke unfair comparisons to husbands everywhere."

- "We interrupt this chick flick because you have cried enough, and your tears pose a significant drowning threat to your family."

- "We interrupt this beauty pageant to bring you a word from the Plastics Council."

- "Due to popular demand from our female viewers, we will not interrupt the following chocolate commercial."

Mom or Grandma?

Women are having babies at older ages than ever before, as evidenced by the fact that every so often there's another story on the news about a woman who gave birth at age fifty-six or sixty-three. One news station recently began its newscast with a story about a woman in her sixties who gave birth to twins!

Women are able to give birth at more advanced ages partly because of new and better fertility drugs. And partly it's the result of women wishing to retain their youth by having children at an age when they'd traditionally be moving to Florida to can fruit.

Last year a sixty-seven-year-old woman gave birth. She was the only one in the delivery room whose Lamaze breathing involved an oxygen mask.

It's a challenge to raise children when you're older. Babies pick up their speech patterns from parents. Do we want a world in which children show up for the first day of preschool saying, "What's good for the goose is good for the gander," or, "We get a milk break? That's the cat's meow!" and complaining about brittle bones, how Social Security is running dry, and how TV Land runs *Green Acres* too late at night? The other preschoolers would tease her mercilessly (using their cell phones to check with their legal defense teams, of course).

I went to school with a kid whose parents were in their midforties when he was born. By the time high school graduation rolled around, his parents, God bless 'em, to us looked like King Tut and Rose Kennedy. Which we all thought was the cat's meow.

The good thing about having a baby later in life, however, is that in most cases, a stroller can give you as much support as a walker; and for us ladies, it can carry a lot more than a purse.

Desperate Grandmas

Grandmas and grandpas have changed a lot over the years. I remember visiting my grandparents almost every summer, and there was a sense about them that was, well, grandmotherly and grandfatherly. My grandmother always wore a housedress. She kept her waist-length hair in a perfect braid that she wrapped around the top of her head. She could make a peach cobbler or strawberry shortcake so delicious that I still dream about them. She even smelled like a grandma, from whatever face powder or talc she used (and probably some of the peach cobbler).

Grandpa was tall and lean and wore a hat much of the time. I remember him taking me for walks in the field behind their home, where he would pick flowers for me. He seemed to always have a beard of stubble, and both he and Grandma were always ready to open their home to whoever came to their door.

I remember taking baths in their metal washtub and eating jellies and vegetables that Grandma had canned. She would quilt, too, and sew, and no matter what else she was doing, she seemed to have all the time in the world to talk to me.

Grandparents today are different. Some are a whole lot different. In what way?

I'm glad you asked.

the **Female Team**

yesterday's **Grandma**	today's **Grandma**
Invites you to her farm for the summer	Calls you from Zimbabwe, where she's serving in the French Foreign Legion
Looks like Aunt Bea	Looks like Cher
Bakes homemade apple pies for you	Orders McDonald's apple pies for you
Hand-crochets a sweater for your birthday	Has her assistant mail you a mall gift certificate for your birthday
Always available to talk to you	Will talk with you right after she gets off her fifth cell-phone call
Reads you a bedtime story	Sends you to bed while she watches *CSI*
Keeps her life savings in coins hidden in a jar at the back of the pantry	Spends your inheritance on a new Harley, a face-lift, and a trip to Bora Bora
Plays checkers with you	Watches *Deal or No Deal* with you
Serves you warm chocolate-chip cookies straight out of the oven	Serves you Keebler's chocolate-chip cookies straight out of the bag
Watches soap operas	Lives a soap opera
Cooks with a cast-iron skillet	Cooks?

You Know You're Getting Older When . . .

- Getting up from a seated position takes longer than it did to go through the tenth grade.

- You watch *Grey's Anatomy* just to jot down the symptoms.

- You try passing off a blood-pressure cuff as an accessory.

- You wonder if a laundry spot remover would work on your face.

- You're retaining enough water to be officially classified as a fire hydrant.

- All the weight you've ever lost over the course of your life has, like the swallows to Capistrano, made a return trip to your waist.

- Your cheeks have seen more slippage than Malibu after a rainstorm.

- You receive a letter from the historical society requesting your childhood photos.

Why Exercise Sometimes Doesn't Work

- It's too hard to do jumping jacks and eat a sundae at the same time.

- Marathons sometimes go past McDonald's, and waiting in the drive-through lane can really cut into your time.

- It's easier to let your pants do the stretching than your muscles.

- You won't be able to get top dollar at your garage sale for that exercise equipment if you actually use it.

- Exercise videos are much more relaxing if you just light an aromatic candle, lie down, close your eyes, and listen to the music.

- A Crunch in candy-bar form takes far less energy than a crunch in the weight-lifting form.

- Pilates really works your abdominal muscles. But so does digesting a third plate of lasagna. Which sounds like more fun to you?

- A treadmill has an Off button.

- Floating takes far less energy than swimming laps. Sinking even less.

- The gym has a snack bar.

Bigger Isn't Always Better

High-definition television may be a wonderful thing for the viewer, but for those who have to appear on it, it's not such a welcome invention. Not only does every laugh line and crow's foot show up, but they show up magnified hundreds of times their actual size. It's like those mirrors we women use to pluck our eyebrows. Would we ever want anyone else seeing us in that kind of magnification? Of course not. That's why we do it in the privacy of our bathrooms, or in our cars while changing lanes.

But movie stars have no choice. They sign contracts that permit the whole world to see their facial pores and every unplucked hair, magnified through high definition. In some instances a star's facial pores can be mistaken for a documentary on black holes. This can't be good for their careers. But it's something they have to deal with.

That's not the only area of life where bigger isn't better.

When it comes to food portions, bigger is usually not better. Just because a turkey is in our freezer doesn't mean we have to cook it and put the whole bird between two slices of bread. We should use three slices of bread and make a double-decker sandwich, of course.

Bigger isn't always better when it comes to diamonds either.

Contrary to what we're led to believe, diamonds aren't a girl's best friend. Her husband, kids, extended family members, friends, and God can be, but not a gem. What good is it to own the Hope Diamond if we've got no one around who loves us unconditionally? Besides, do you know the kind of carpal tunnel you'd get from wearing a rock like that?

Bigger isn't always better when it comes to shopping malls. They're fun to visit, but when you just want to run in and buy a cute new pair of shoes, you don't want to have to walk across two state lines to do it.

A few things, though, do seem better when we supersize them:

- Contentment

- Laughter

- Love

- Forgiveness

- Grace

- Peace

- Hope

- Gratitude

- Faith

- And, of course, chocolate

Ten Stupid Things Women Boomers Do to Mess Up Their Lives

- Volunteer to watch all five grandchildren on the first day of their chickenpox outbreak.

- Hit twelve consecutive outlet malls and not recall at which one they left their husband.

- Ride the triple upside-down loop-d-loop roller coaster with their granddaughter. Twice. After eating two orders of jalapeño nachos.

- Wear panty hose that have lost their elasticity around people who have lost their sense of humor.

- Sit on the floor in a cross-legged position for longer than twenty minutes, unless planning on giving their blood circulation the weekend off.

- Fail to put lock on the thermostat during menopause.

- Allow husband to buy electric blanket during menopause.

- Sign up for assertiveness training during menopause.

- Put car keys and glasses anywhere but around their neck.

- Attempt to break the limbo record at their thirtieth high school reunion.

The Black Hole of Passwords

We have passwords for everything these days. We have credit card passwords, phone message passwords, computer passwords, e-mail passwords . . . so many numbers are bouncing around in our brains, it's no wonder we find ourselves banging our heads on the ATM machine trying to remember if our password is our youngest child's birth year minus our age, or if it's the number of our grandchildren multiplied by the number of years we've been married.

To help boomer women with all the different numbers we have to keep in mind these days, here are some tips for coming up with passwords. These are easy-to-remember but hard-to-break passwords that you can feel free to use:

- The number of hairs left on your head multiplied by the average number of leg cramps you get per night

- The number of stones surgically removed from your gallbladder plus the year of your last MRI

- The number of pills you have to take per day for your acid reflux times the number of grandchildren you have

- The year you graduated from high school divided by how many of your teeth are still your own—plus your middle name

- The length of your husband's comb-over (in inches) subtracted from the age of your pet multiplied by the number of varicose veins on your right leg

- Your home address plus the first three digits of your Social Security number (assuming there are more than three digits in your Social Security number)

- The highest number of tacos you've ever eaten in one sitting subtracted from the highest number of antacids that followed, plus your nickname in high school

- The number of age spots on your left hand (rounded up to the closest even number) multiplied by the number of times your neighbor parked on your lawn last year

- Your anniversary year divided by the average number of hours of uninterrupted sleep you get per night due to your husband's snoring, plus the name Hugo

- The number of hours of Dr. Phil you've watched this week divided by the names of the winning team of the last season of *Dancing with the Stars*

Implement the tips above when choosing your next password, and you'll never again be locked out of your e-mail, voice mail, or banking system. But you might want to carry around a copy of this book for reference.

A Million Isn't What It Used to Be

Question: does winning a million dollars sound as good as it did forty years ago? Don't get me wrong. I'd still cash the check. But a million dollars just doesn't seem to have the same ring to it that it once did. Consider the following comparison:

what a **Million Dollars Used to Buy**	what a **Million Dollars Can Still Buy**
The wedding gown of your dreams	The wedding rice of your dreams
The finest crystal from Waterford	The finest cups from Dixie
A diamond necklace	A candy necklace
A shopping spree on Rodeo Drive	Four grocery items at the minimart
A mansion in California	A trailer in Boise
A European vacation	A basket of French croissants, German potato salad, and half an Italian sausage
A three-week ocean voyage	A one-hour paddle-boat ride
An island	Thousand Island dressing
A comfortable retirement	A comfortable robe
Elvis to sing at your birthday party	William Hung to sing at your birthday party

The Race Goes On

Things We Still Don't Know
After All These Years

If we're living life right, we're supposed to get smarter over time. We make mistakes and learn our lessons. We try one thing, and if it doesn't work, we try something else. We pick wrong friends and learn to pick better ones next time. We grow. We mature. For most women, time is our teacher.

But time doesn't answer all of our questions. Some things we still don't know after all these years—things that baffled us in our youth or young adult years and are still baffling us today. Times may change, but these mysteries haven't, and I don't know about you, but as a woman I would really like to know the answer to the following:

- Just what was it that Billy Joe McAlister threw off the Tallahatchie Bridge?

- Are the single socks we lose in the washing machine the same single socks I find by the curb while jogging? (This is obviously a trick question. Me? Jog?)

the **Female Team**

- Why did it take Susan Lucci so long to win a Daytime Emmy Award?

- Why are we called the weaker sex when some of us have been known to give birth to six babies in the same day?

- What in the world was Seinfeld thinking with that final show?

- What does compounded interest really mean, and why does it amount to only four cents on my savings account statement?

- What is the correct translation of "Do wah diddy diddy dum diddy do"?

- Who really shot J.R.? I'm still not buying the dream thing.

- What is Cool Whip made of, and why does it never melt?

- Just how tan can George Hamilton get before being officially considered deep-fried?

Head Knowledge

In my head I still have the same body I had back in high school. (Sometimes I have to close my eyes to pull this off, but I do what I have to do.) When I picture myself running, the vision I get isn't the gasping, wheezing, leg-cramping woman who always shows up in reality. In my head, I'm a muscle-toned athlete winning a marathon. In my head, I easily come in first place in the Ladies Professional Golf Association Tour. In reality, I can't even find where they're playing the LPGA Tour. The bottom line is, sports and exercise have a completely different outcome in reality than what I picture in my head.

In My Head I Can . . .	In Reality I Can . . .
Jump rope for twenty minutes	Jump rope for two minutes and then spend the next hour and a half trying to get myself untangled
Get drafted for the Women's Baseball League	Sell candy bars for Little League
Easily squeeze through a tight turnstile	Stay perfectly still as the nice firemen cut me free after getting stuck in a tight turnstile
Read the small print in a phone book	Call Directory Assistance
Jog a mile	Drive a mile
Work out with a personal trainer	Have lunch with a personal trainer
Jump on a trampoline	Jump through a trampoline
Play in a tennis match	Light a fireplace match
Do the limbo	Live in limbo
Burn the midnight oil	Burn the Deep Heat ointment
Do ten leg lifts	Do ten leg scratches
Fit into my wedding gown again	Fit into my wedding gloves again

Making Our Voices Heard

They say the best way to affect change in society is by making our voices heard. We can do that by voting, attending town-hall meetings, writing to our political leaders, and basically just being involved. In previous books I've suggested a Million Menopausal Women March to let Congress and the president know our concerns as hot-flashing baby boomers. Until we can organize this march, I thought I would use this forum to make a few suggestions on how we, as baby boomer women, can make our voices heard.

Sit-In

Remember the sit-ins of the 1960s? This would be similar, only we'd bring along our La-Z-Boys. We can protest without being uncomfortable.

No-Hunger Strike

Gandhi had his hunger strike, but our strike would be a no-hunger strike. In fact, we would refuse to stop eating until they offered us an audience with the president. They could never outlast us. We're so committed to our cause, we'd be willing to keep eating indefinitely.

Peace March

Ours would be like other peace marches, only we'd do it on moving sidewalks to save energy.

Running for Office

If we don't like how things are going, why not run for office ourselves? Look at Ronald Reagan. They told him he was too old, but he ignored them and won anyway. Twice.

Getting Close

So how are we doing? Have we found it yet? Did the women's team discover the whereabouts of the elusive Fountain of Youth? Or were we right from the get-go: the Fountain of Youth isn't something tangible but something inside each of us, available only to those wise enough to recognize it.

In any case, the men still get their turn to search. But even if a Fountain of Youth did exist, I don't think I'd want them to find it. Not just because I'd want our side to win, either. I'm not at all sure I'd want to live in a world where no one ever got older. And wiser.

Here's what I believe a world without birthday candles and antiwrinkle cream would look like:

Every time you faced a problem in your life, you'd have no choice but to seek the shallow advice of the seventeen-year-old next door who knows everything but has lived through nothing.

Marital problems? "Dump him, girlfriend! Don't waste any time working together or on your own issues—just move on to the next guy. Why get married anyway? That's so old-fashioned. For better or for worse? Puh-leeease."

Financial problems? "You're broke? Here's another credit-card application. Let's go shopping. It'll make you feel better! And buy me something so I can feel better, too."

The Race Goes On

If we ever had unlimited access to a youth-giving fountain, we would never access the wisdom that comes with age, because true wisdom doesn't develop overnight. It comes with time, experience, and being mature enough to surrender what we think is a good plan to what God knows is the best plan. Without this kind of wisdom, we would all stay shallow forever.

And who would control the newly discovered Fountain of Youth? If it fell into the wrong hands, it could be used as leverage to gain worldwide dominance. We'd never get to watch *Lost* or *24* or any of our favorite TV shows. The television would be interminably set to Nickelodeon.

A Fountain of Youth would affect other elements of society, too. Here are just a few of the things that would change if anyone succeeded in discovering this legendary fountain.

- Clairol revenues would be cut in half.

- Little Red Riding Hood would have no place to visit.

- Glasses of water the world over would have no teeth in them.

- Twelve would be the new middle age.

- Many of us would never know what talc smells like.

- We'd no longer have a slow lane on freeways. Who'd drive in it?

- We wouldn't get senior discounts.

- A lot fewer cookies would be homemade.

- Cruise ship companies would be forced to go out of business.

- "Quilting? What's that?"

- Grandkids would miss out on a healthy dose of spoiling.

We can all keep searching for the Fountain of Youth, but something tells me if we ever find it, if we ever have the ability to keep the world from growing older and reaping benefits that come with that, we will have lost a lot.

running **Neck and Neck:**

Obstacles and Racing Tips for Both the Male and Female Teams

Some situations and strategies, complications and hurdles, apply to both male and female teams. That's why we're providing this section for both the middle-aged man and the middle-aged woman. In these areas, the race to the Fountain of Youth challenges us all.

Upside and Downside
of Turning Fifty

Downside	Upside
Hair loss	10 percent AARP discount on rental cars
Potential heart disease	
Aching joints	
Increased risk of diabetes, high blood pressure, and emphysema	
General fatigue	
General sense of boredom with same-old same-old	
Increased tooth decay	
Overall malaise, a looming sense of our own mortality	

Signs Your Eyesight
Could Be Worsening

- You kiss the mailman and hand your spouse a postcard to be mailed.

- You list your favorite book of the year as *The Ba Vinci Code*.

- You send your grandkid to school wearing the dog's sweater.

- You drive to work in reverse.

- Not only can you not read a newspaper, but now you can no longer locate the newspaper on the front porch.

- You can no longer locate the front porch.

Working Till We Drop

Both men and women are now working much longer than earlier generations did, many continuing to toil well beyond the standard retirement age. This is partly because many of us feel working keeps us young, vibrant, and alive. But mostly it's because the average person's retirement savings is two dollars and fourteen cents. Toss in the perception that Social Security is as reliable as a 1978 Pinto with two hundred thousand miles on it being driven by an illegal immigrant without a license across the Rocky Mountains during a blizzard without snow tires, and many feel compelled to continue punching a time clock through their sixties and even into their seventies or eighties.

Whatever the reasons, it's becoming more common to see older people hard at work. A New Yorker named Hoy Wong recently celebrated his ninetieth birthday on the job. No truth to the rumor that his favorite drink includes something called a "Metamucil chaser."

I (Brad) recently encountered a taxi driver who must've been in his early eighties. He drove me home from the airport at fifteen miles per hour with his turn signal on. That's the last time I get in a cab with a bumper sticker reading, "Ask me about my great-grandchild." This driver was so old school, he actually spoke a few words of English.

Because workers are retiring later, here are some suggestions for workplace changes that would help accommodate the graying workforce.

- Trade the office water cooler for an office prune-juice cooler.

- Replace the traditional coffee break with an Ensure break.

- Trade holiday bonus for "Glad You Made It Another Year" stipend.

- Replace traditional two-week summer vacation with two-week employee cruise and *Lawrence Welk Show* reunion.

- Desk chairs—out. Rockers—in.

- Instead of Employee of the Month status, give special recognition and parking space for October's Grand Geezer.

- Instead of name tags, provide workers with Life Alert pendants.

- Paying retirement benefits is passé. Paying funeral expenses is "in."

- Replace the company softball team with a company croquet team.

- Exchange executive lunchroom privileges for Meals on Wheels.

- Change annual corporate retreat to a three-day nap in the woods.

As long as we're all working longer, companies should do what they can to accommodate us—even if that means implementing Take Your Great-granddaughter to Work Day.

Acting Their Age

As some of our favorite actors enter their middle and senior years, Hollywood will no doubt start offering these great talents different kinds of roles. Not that their acting abilities have diminished in the least. It's just that, well, that's show biz . . .

New Opportunities for Older Actors	
Actor	**Starring In**
Bruce Willis	*Dye Hard*
Phyllis Diller	*Extreme Makeover: Hopeless Edition*
Clint Eastwood	*The Bridges of Madison Dental Clinic*
Warren Beatty	*Shampoo (For Toupees Only)*
Burt Reynolds	*Cannonball Walk*
Michael Keaton	*Batgrandpa*
Mel Gibson	*What Boomers Want*
Doris Roberts	*Everybody Loves Oat Bran*
Kevin Costner	*Dances with Gout*
Julie Andrews	*The Sound of Indigestion*

Custom Exercise Equipment and Clothing for the Baby Boomer

Companies have realized that the boomer generation is a shopping force like none other. Hence they have begun a marketing plan like none other, especially in the exercise equipment and clothing industries. Here are just a few of the new products that will soon be offered to us:

The Pirates Cot

Like the Pilates mat, the Pirates (pronounced *Pi-rah-tees)* cot gives you not only an exercise mat but also a comfortable cot to sleep on while watching your Pilates workout videos. It comes with an eye patch to go along with the pirate (pronounced *pie-rate)* theme that's so popular today. The patch also helps you focus on one side of your body at a time—a plus in any personal trainer's book.

Charlie the Tuna Workout System

Like Nautilus exercise equipment, the Charlie the Tuna exercise machine works several of your muscles simultaneously. From the opening of the can to the draining and scooping out of the tuna, this system will give baby boomers like us just the exercise program we've been waiting for.

The Possum

Like the Tony Little Gazelle exercise machine, the Possum also works on the principle of moving like a wild animal to lose weight. Not as fast as a gazelle, the possum moves at a safer, more accommodating speed. The Possum exercise machine mimics the possum's movements. It even has a Nap mode for those who prefer an even slower pace. If that's still too fast, try the Road Kill setting.

Wet Blanket Weightlifting

Anyone can lift weights to build muscle; but if you really want a good workout, try transferring a wet blanket from the washer to the dryer four or five times a day. You'll end up with muscles like a bodybuilder—and cleaner blankets, too.

Stationary Tricycle

The stationary tricycle is a smaller version of the stationary bicycle, designed to reduce the risk of injury and make it easier to mount and dismount. The stationary tricycle is revolutionary in that it affords users the circular motion of a bicycle for their feet and legs to tone and work vital muscles, but it also gives you something extra: a little horn and handlebar tassels to play with.

When you consider that the number-one reason middle-agers give for not exercising is boredom, the stationary tricycle might be the perfect solution.

Cross-Country (Music) Skiing Machine

While this boomer equipment is similar to a regular cross-country skiing machine, ours differs in one area: the workout music. Imagine country music legends cheering you on to tunes like:

- "(I Got) Pains in Low Places"

- "Ring of Bengay"

- "I Walk the Treadmill"

- "Napping 9 to 5"

- "If You've Got the Money, I've Got the Medical Bills"

- "Breathe (and Gasp and Wheeze)"

- "There Drops My Everything"

Treadmill with Paramedic Attachment

Let's be honest with ourselves. If you've lived a sedentary lifestyle, and who among us hasn't, do you really think it's wise to purchase an ordinary treadmill without a personal paramedic attached? Of course not. As far as we know, we're the first to suggest such an accessory. None of the better-known exercise equipment companies are meeting this very real need.

Thigh-Thinner Shorts

You've heard about exercise equipment guaranteed to give you firmer, sleeker thighs in just a few short weeks. But all of those machines require some sort of exertion on your part. Not our thigh thinner. The secret to our baby boomer thigh thinner is optical illusion. Our patented Thigh-Thinner Shorts (available for $79.99) squeeze unwanted thigh flesh into—are you ready for this?—the cellulite indentations that are already there! It's sort of like packing the contents of a four-bedroom house into a ten-foot trailer. To make it work, you've got to find all the empty holes and pockets, right? It's the same with our shorts. They find all those cellulite "holes" that are taking up unnecessary space and giving your thighs the illusion of being bigger than they really are. Our shorts fill those holes and give your thighs a thinner, sleeker appearance.

Rowing Machine with Guide

Would you ever in your right mind canoe down unfamiliar rapids by yourself? Of course not! You'd be risking your life! It's the same with working out on a rowing machine. Don't go it alone! This rowing machine comes with its own personal guide—a muscular type who not only can row till the cows come home but can speak four languages, two of them heretofore believed to be lost tongues. Let our experienced guide do all the rowing while you just ride along and enjoy the trip. No pain: no kidding!

Exercise Tennis Ball

Similar to the giant ball used in health clubs across the nation, the Exercise Tennis Ball works the same muscles, but with virtually no risk of injury (due to the fact that should you fall, it would only be a three-inch drop).

Stair Stepper with Escalator Attachment

Works the same as a regular stair stepper, only this one offers the ease of an escalator system. Sure, it's only a couple of steps, but why risk overexertion and leg cramps? The escalator attachment is easily removable for when company comes and you want your friends to think you're the athletic type. When they leave, simply reattach the escalator accessory, and you're good to go.

Collectible Hits and Misses

The following is a list of things that some of us women have kept through the years, as well as some things we probably didn't need to bother with:

was **Worth Keeping**	was not **Worth Keeping**
Miniskirt from the seventies	Mini-Wheats from the eighties
The Munsters trading cards from the sixties	Chewing gum that came with *The Munsters* trading cards from the sixties
Elvis movie script	Script from *My Mother the Car*
Superman comic book #1	Superman comic book #4,503,327
Original Brady Bunch lunch box	Original lunch from the Brady Bunch lunch box
Barbie doll in original packaging	Right arm and one shoe from Barbie doll
Concert tickets for The Beatles	Concert tickets for Bart's Band
Newspaper with headline "Man Goes to Moon"	Newspaper with headline "Man Watches Lunar Eclipse"
Poodle skirt from 1959	Dog biscuit from 1962
Original Andy Warhol painting	Original paint-by-numbers painting, unfinished
Signed cast photo from *Star Trek*	Signed cast from broken toe sustained in sixth-grade dodgeball game
Personal letter from Ronald Reagan	Dukakis poster
Backstage pass from The Supremes' Farewell tour	Backstage pass from International Summit on Warts
Oscar purchased from the Mary Pickford estate sale	Bowling trophy, missing arm with ball, bought at Goober's yard sale
Crowd photo of John F. Kennedy's motorcade in Dallas on the day he was shot: could shed light on conspiracy theories	"Who Killed J.R.?" bumper sticker, torn
Deed to Texas oil field left to you by your great-uncle Ebenezer	Deeds to Reading Railroad and St. Charles Place: that's all that's left of your circa 1963 Monopoly game

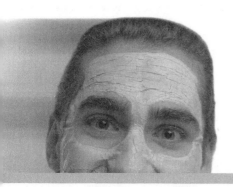

the **Male Team**

by **Brad Dickson**

Growing older ain't easy. Somewhere around age forty, fifty if he's lucky, a man realizes he can no longer stay up until 3:00 a.m., avoiding exercise and consuming a diet built around the four "staples"—chips, dip, peanut butter, and corn dogs. The man realizes that his body converts everything he eats to fat before he gets up from the table. The man notices his body no longer functions as it once did—that some parts are deteriorating, that his metabolism is slower than Congress, and that his joints (especially his knees) are about as flexible as mahogany. He realizes he can't perform difficult, herculean tasks—like using a stapler—without throwing out his back. He has an epiphany that if he were a car, his warranty would've expired fifty thousand miles ago. He wakes up one morning and it dawns on him that he has more yesterdays than tomorrows.

Some men are taking an acute, active interest in their health and well-being by doing whatever they can to stay young. An estimated 12 percent of all plastic surgeries last year were performed on men. It used to be that the only time a man even considered plastic surgery was when he ran into a wall or flew through a windshield.

Although better informed than in the past, many men today are fearful. Fearful of getting fat, of losing hair, of growing old, of dying. So some change their diets, get hair plugs, or think about joining a gym. But they rarely go to the doctor for a physical—most men are deathly afraid to go.

But the times are definitely a-changin'. Many companies are seeking to capitalize on men's concerns about growing older by coming out with lines of skin-care products and antiaging elixirs just for men. Pretty much every company but Pep Boys presently has a line of skin-care products for guys, and Pep Boys is probably working on one. Some men spend large sums of money on these products in hopes of staying young.

Do our methods for staying young work? Some do; many don't. To compensate for the ones that don't, we've developed a series of coping mechanisms to delude ourselves into believing we're still young. Before you can take positive action, you must first notice the warning signs that you are, in fact, aging.

Red Flags That Warn a Man He's Getting Older

- You watch a *Brady Bunch* rerun, and instead of Peter Brady, you suddenly identify with Sam the Butcher.

- You buy a convertible for its "youth appeal" and are shocked to notice sixty people on a passing bus simultaneously pointing and laughing at your hair plugs.

- You have your first date with a woman who says you remind her of her dad, only you're grayer.

- You spend two-thirds of your free time perusing pamphlets for devices (with names like "Super Belly-Deflater") to decrease the size of your gut.

- Once a week your wife gathers all the hair from your shower drain into two lawn bags she sets out by the curb.

- The trash collectors refuse to take the above bags because they're too heavy.

- The "oldies" radio station is playing songs from when you were in your midthirties.

- Your teeth are the same color as a Yield sign.

- The only place you can hear all your favorite songs is on the supermarket PA system.

- You allot an extra four minutes to getting ready in the morning so you can shave your ears.

- You're above the median age at a Beach Boys concert, which is the same thing as being above the median age in a cemetery.

- You lose the TV remote in a crease in your forehead.

- You set your alarm for 4:00 a.m. so you can watch the infomercial for guys who are going bald.

- You have to replace the bedroom carpet you wore out going to the bathroom in the middle of the night.

- Men around forty start referring to you as "Pops."

- You gain twenty pounds in six months—all in your prostate.

- Older people are even starting to look young to you. For example, you keep mistaking Larry King for Ryan Seacrest.

- Instead of chocolate, your last birthday cake was oat bran.

- All your favorite programs are on TV Land.

Health

Fear and Loathing in the Waiting Room

I'd like to get something off my chest—I loathe physicians. *Loathe* may not be the correct term. I respect many doctors for their professionalism and education, so maybe a more appropriate word is *fear.* They have all the power in the relationship. If I go to a mechanic and he tells me my brake pads are shot, I know just enough about brake pads to fake a rebuttal. If a doctor tells me my gallbladder is diseased, well, what can I do except don the hospital gown and take my medicine? This is why men avoid doctors as if doctors were the plague, or a wedding. If we suspect something is wrong, we attempt to diagnose ourselves. We go to the library or get online to discover what ails us.

Case in point: A couple years ago I suddenly noticed little red spots all over my body. Being a hypochondriac of mythic proportions, I immediately diagnosed myself as suffering from Red Spotted Fever, spread, of course, by the East African tick found on porcupines in remote sections of Mozambique.

Not wanting to risk infecting others, in lieu of calling the doctor, I dug out the old mask I wore during the anticipated SARS epidemic a few years ago and drove to the bookstore. I immersed myself in a medical encyclopedia and soon discovered that the red spots were something called "cherry angiomas." They're an annoyance that suddenly appears when you reach middle age, like the AARP magazine.

I'm not alone. Many men have an aversion to physicians. Doctors should be a vital part of a man's health and antiaging program. But most men are more likely to ask a cab driver for health and antiaging advice than they are their doctor. (Assuming men even have a doctor. If pressed to name my personal physician, I'd have to say the last doctor I went to on a regular basis was Dr. Mitchell—my pediatrician.)

When men are sick, they rationalize that they don't need a doctor. We usually blame our malady on "something I ate." In the ambulance on the way to the hospital with crushing chest pains, a guy will say, "I guess I learned my lesson. That's the last time I eat two-day-old spaghetti!"

Day three in the cardiac care unit, a guy will confess: "That lasagna obviously did not agree with me, doc. Give me a shot and I'll be on my way. I gotta be more careful what I shove down my throat."

Among the most common last words for a man are, "I'll feel better as soon as this tuna works its way through my system."

Health

We regularly blame illness on the wrong choice of food or beverage. At a wake for a mutual friend, all the men will exchange knowing glances. "It was the bratwurst."

This is why men feel they never have to go to the doctor. The answer to most illnesses is to let the offending food work its way through our intestines. Actually, that's not quite correct. A man is willing to go to the doctor if he, say, loses a limb or needs a kidney or a heart—provided it's an outpatient procedure.

With the possible exception of being audited or attending a trombone recital featuring twenty five-year-olds playing "Lady of Spain," a man hates nothing more than going to the doctor. Although I'm willing if the cab driver doesn't get back to me soon with that second opinion.

He Died of *What*?

Because men avoid doctors, occasionally one of us gets a rude awakening. That's what happened to a friend of mine, Alex.

Until I heard about Alex, I'd only lost friends to accidents. That all changed in 2002.

At my first funeral for a friend who succumbed to natural causes, I felt bad for him and his family, but at the same time, all the guys were whispering, "A heart attack. Alex died of natural causes?! He was about my age. I guess I'm getting up there. Why couldn't he have fallen off a cliff in Maui?"

It was horrible learning of Alex's death. He wasn't an extremely close friend, but we'd run in the same circle for years. I felt bad for him. For all of us in that circle. As baby boomers, we routinely embarrass ourselves by doing things like bungee jumping and skydiving and disco dancing to ABBA records, so we're used to hearing about injuries, accidents, and dismemberments among our fellows. But now we were at an age at which we were eligible to die from natural causes.

After the funeral, we lined up to talk to his wife and express our condolences while subtly trying to elicit information. "Sorry about your loss. . . . Did he look ill? Did his tongue turn this color? Ahhhhhh!"

It was a traumatic time, because as baby boomers we think

we're younger than we really are. When one of us succumbs to natural causes, it's a real shock.

Contrary to conventional wisdom, men do put stock in the latest medical studies and advances. We want to know if something can kill us. Many men I know took interest in a new study last year announcing that the bad condition of your teeth and gums can lead to premature death. I question this survey. If bad teeth led to premature death, the average life span in Britain would be twelve years.

One problem is that when you're over forty, there's a good chance the doctor will be younger than you. In most every man's life, there's a moment of epiphany when he's sitting on the table in the doctor's office in his thirteen-year-old underwear with the hole roughly the same size as the one in the ozone layer, thinking he should've worn the good stuff, the eleven-year-old underwear, and expecting a distinguished-looking doctor resembling Marcus Welby to enter the room, when in walks a guy who looks like Haley Joel Osment in a lab coat.

The male patient immediately recoils, realizing the undershorts he's wearing are older than the doctor.

What does this kid know? When I was his age, I was locking myself out of my car at spring break. And he's going to tell me what's wrong with me? I don't think so.

Distrust of doctors, combined with the fact that as you age, more things can go wrong, makes the entire going-to-the-doctor experience one men dread. As you get older, you essentially turn into the human version of an '88 Yugo, and when there's a problem, sometimes the parts just aren't available.

the **Male Team**

Many men fear the doctor because, worst-case scenario, a doctor can tell you that you won't long be among the living. But death isn't the main reason I fear getting older. What I fear most are the changing expectations society places on us as we age. See the following age chart and how society has designated what you should be doing at that stage of your life.

the **Various Life Stage**	
Birth to age 5:	The toilet experimentation years.
Ages 5–10:	The sticking foreign objects into your nose and mouth years
11–18:	The pimply years
18–19:	The work at McDonald's years
20–30:	The ruin your hearing by listening to loud, awful music years
30–40:	The learning to change a diaper years
40–50:	The distended belly years
50–60:	The "My job was outsourced and all I got was this lousy T-shirt" years
60–70:	The start to think about paying back those college student loan years
70–80:	The golden retirement years
80–100:	The go back to work at McDonald's years

Still, boomer guys can reject what society dictates we should be doing at a certain age. After all, we sometimes delude ourselves into believing we're twenty years old. Until one day our bodies say, "Hey—stop lying, old guy."

Denial Is Not Just a River

Most men are in a constant state of denial regarding their health. That's because although they wish to stay young and healthy and live forever, men are terrified of doctors. I've seen guys face extremely frightening things—like war and watching *The View*—without batting an eye; yet they're petrified at the thought of going to a medical professional, or even an HMO. Even though they know seeing a doctor is a good idea if you want to prolong life and keep feeling young and healthy, they still figure it's not worth it. And you really can't blame them for their trepidation. A doctor once told me my blood pressure was 165 over 100 and put me on medication. This doctor then sent me two pamphlets informing me that high blood pressure is the "silent killer," which made my blood pressure spike up to 180 over 105. One more pamphlet in the mail and I probably wouldn't even be here today.

What also didn't help was the fact that this doctor had the bedside manner of a professional wrestler. And not a nice professional wrestler, but one of those who wear masks and throw other guys off the turnbuckle. This doctor was as stone-faced as a Secret Service agent and as tactful as a rodeo clown. So I became proactive, which is always a good idea when it comes to your health.

the Male Team

I bought a home monitor, which told me that my true blood pressure was 121 over 78. I thought perhaps the device was faulty, so I purchased a second monitor that did, in fact, reveal the first to be faulty. My true pressure was 118 over 67.

As with exercise guidelines, the medical profession recently changed the guidelines for what constitutes healthy blood pressure, making the standards stricter and more complex. Which means the guidelines we've been following for the past eight hundred years are wrong. Below is a chart showing the old and the revised blood pressure standards.

Old Standard

Systolic under 140:....... Normal

Systolic over 140: .... High

(Systolic is a medical term meaning "something to do with blood pressure.")

New Standard

Systolic under 120:....... Normal

Systolic 120–130:......... Could be problematic

Systolic 130–135:......... Uh-oh

Systolic 135–137.5:....... Geez . . .

Systolic 137.5–138:...... Whoa!

Systolic 138–139:......... AHHHHHH!

Systolic over 140: .... "Predeath"

The bottom blood pressure number is referred to as *diastolic,* a word whose meaning is unknown even to trained physicians.

I'm going to throw a term at you that explains many cases of high blood pressure. That term is "white coat hypertension." White coat hypertension is defined as an ailment wherein the moment the cuff goes around your arm in the doctor's office, numbers appear that resemble the average American credit score.

When I see a doctor with a blood pressure monitor, my body reacts the way most people would if they saw a ghost with a chainsaw coming at them. I suffer from white coat hypertension so severe that I can't watch *Grey's Anatomy* without convulsing on the floor. If I see a commercial for a product called the Rug Doctor, I break out in hives. I had to quit watching cartoons because of the phrase, "What's up, Doc?"

The good news is, being afraid of doctors and having white coat hypertension won't kill me. I just have to avoid regular checkups.

Why I Distrust Doctors

Actually, I do get regular checkups—every time the Comet Kohoutek makes an appearance or the Democrats win the White House, I'm there. I wait until after a mole has grown to the size of the former planet Pluto to get it checked. When I'm walking down the street and trip over an overgrown mole on my back, I call the doctor. When neighbor kids start using my skin tags as jump ropes, I make an appointment.

If I have a medical problem, I usually tell myself, I'll just go to an online doctor. That nice guy in India, Dr. Ajay, who prescribed the sleeping medication I bought from the online pharmacy in New Delhi—he'll know what to do about the mole. If I call today, he'll probably send something in the mail tomorrow, as long as I include eight dollars for the medication and $39.95 for "shipping." He'll probably also be able to solve my computer problem: I'll kill two birds with one stone.

I don't trust doctors because they know many things I don't. And men don't like people who know things we don't. I've never met Stephen Hawking, and I respect him for his accomplishments, yet I don't like him. He knows things I don't. Many things.

Another big reason I and many other men distrust doctors

more than ever is that they have recently discovered new, innovative ways of charging for services that have been free since the day golf was invented and God created doctors to fill the courses. Many physicians are now charging for "services" such as calling the pharmacy, photocopying medical records, and filling out forms. At this rate we can soon look forward to the specimen-jar tax and the rubber-glove surcharge. The next time a surgeon leaves a pair of scissors inside a patient, the patient will receive a bill charging him for the scissors.

Of course, it's necessary for doctors today to charge exorbitant fees, as they must buy medical malpractice insurance that's equal to the gross national product of Chile. This insurance is mandatory because of all the wacky patients filing frivolous lawsuits against physicians for such trivial things as amputating the wrong leg.

And when a doctor does make an honest mistake, such as confusing two patients and removing the lung from the guy who went in for a hip replacement and vice versa, juries typically award the injured party something in the vicinity of nine trillion dollars. Plus bus fare.

Still, consider the doctor's visit from the man's point of view to realize what a truly miserable experience this is. First he must spend time sitting in a waiting room frequently full of sick people coughing up phlegm the length of airport runways. Then he must get undressed and wait in his underwear in a room that's usually the temperature of Outer Siberia. If they want to make a man comfortable, they should let him sit in his underwear in a warm room with a recliner, big-screen TV tuned to a game, pool table, chips, and a woman in a muumuu shouting at him to do yard work—then the man will feel at home.

After waiting in his underwear, which the man usually doesn't notice is torn and older than Roman numerals until he's half nude in the doctor's office, a stranger—that is, the "doctor"—walks in. The male patient was expecting the doctor to be middle-aged like him; but the doctor is so young, he seems like an embryo with a stethoscope attached.

The embryo looks the man up and down and begins scribbling notes on a page. Notes that the man (the gender that likes to be in control at all times) is not allowed to see. These notes may lead to the man's spending time in the hospital. But the man is powerless to do anything about the notes. Which drives the man out of his mind.

Then, frequently, the man is told he is doing something wrong regarding his health. Men hate being told they're doing something wrong. If doctors want our repeat business, they should focus on and commend the male patient for the few things he is doing right—even if that amounts to, "I've noticed from reading your chart that you're not quite deceased yet."

These few words of encouragement will help the male develop trust in doctors. Which doctors will probably take advantage of by assessing a trust fee.

The Executive Physical

Occasionally, some brave men will set aside their fear and distrust of the medical profession and actually get a physical. Right now, so-called "executive physicals" are all the rage. An executive physical is basically a dressed-up regular physical exam, with extras like diet and exercise recommendations, and is more detailed than a regular exam. An executive physical can save a man's life by catching things a routine physical may miss. But, more important, you check in the night before, and they have free valet parking! (Men will agree to be eaten by sharks if there's free valet parking.)

An executive physical can cost more than a down payment for a home in the Midwest. At eight thousand dollars plus, with a conservative return of 7 percent, in a few years, that eight grand could be worth some real money.

For the executive physical, you go to a wing of a hospital whose lobby would resemble a Four Seasons hotel if Four Seasons had the stench of Bengay strong enough to drop a horse and lots of older guys in hospital gowns and black dress shoes in the lobby. It looks like a formal dance at the ICU.

Regarding the overall concept of the executive physical— learning about potential problems before they emerge—I don't want to know! Unless a bone is protruding through my kneecap, it must not really be broken, so don't fix it. Denial is better than "Dead Middle-Aged Man Walking." Maybe I have something seriously wrong with my body, but as long as it's not bothering me, don't tell me. I'm just fine. Like my credit card balance, I'll deal with it down the road.

The new body scans, which composed a large percentage of my executive physical, have me particularly frightened. They supposedly predict what could happen at some point in the future. They're the medical equivalent of the Amazing Kreskin. I'm here to debunk these scans. I'm more than slightly skeptical of their reliability. Since we don't have the technology to predict what the weather will be like, say, tomorrow, how can anyone possibly tell me what my health will be like in twenty years?

After checking in the night before my executive physical, to "clean out my system," I was given a foul-tasting liquid that turned out to be the colonic equivalent of Mount St. Helens. If not for the free valet parking, I would've been out of there.

After the actual exam, which is eerily similar to any other physical—only more detailed and twenty-six times more expensive—I met with a nutritionist who inquired about my diet.

I also met with an exercise physiologist to whom I lied through my teeth and claimed that I actually followed the government's recommendation to exercise for thirty minutes every day. He looked at me as if I'd just told him I was the

Lindbergh baby. But he earnestly wrote it down and complimented me on my work ethic.

Then it was time to meet with the physicians who had performed the actual executive physical. Feeling like an astronaut who just returned from nine months on the International Space Station, I met my executive physical team—the cardiologist, the nutritionist, the eye man, the guy who specializes in little toes, the left knee expert, and the right armpit guy. The reports were generally positive; however, the doctor who performed the sonic testing said, "Something was slightly off on the X-ray—a slight buildup of plaque, I presume—I don't know for certain, but it's not a problem right now. We can't do anything for it, really . . ."

Really? Then don't tell me! Want me to die of worry? A buildup of what, exactly? Cholesterol? Peanut butter? Antifreeze? He couldn't tell me. So why be such an alarmist? Ever hear of the guy who cried wolf? Imagine Paul Revere riding through the streets shouting, "The British may come someday! The British may come someday!"

The way I look at my health is the way most Americans view the national debt—we'll worry about it some other time.

My executive physical took place eighteen months ago, and thus far the plaque buildup hasn't resulted in any problems I'm aware of—other than my occasional worry-induced insomnia and stress-related atrial fibrillation.

Hypochondria (Or Why I'm Pretty Sure I've Contracted Western Spotted Elk Diphtheria)

I was reassured by my executive physical that I'm basically sound. As I've said previously, I tend to be a hypochondriac. After reading various articles and watching too many episodes of *Dateline,* the local news, and *ER,* at one time or another I thought I'd contracted each of the following ailments and maladies:

- Adult measles

- Lou Gehrig's disease

- Legionnaires' disease

- Bird flu (twice)

- SARS

- E. coli (four times)

- Mad cow disease

- Mad walrus disease

- Chickenpox

- Terminal itchiness

- Monkeypox

- Skunkpox

- Scleroderma

- Hantavirus

- Munchausen syndrome by proxy

- Vitiligo

- Rumsfelditis

- Mulepox

- Lyme disease

- Pig fever

- West Nile virus

- Blimpphobia

- Postpartum depression

- Salmonella

- Bubonic plague

- Gerbilpox

- Equine-induced amnesia

- Sickle cell anemia

- Terminal cooties

- Outer Mongolian diphtheria

- Parvo

The U.S. Health-Care System (Or Why I'm Looking at Property in Canada)

I believe that more American men, even nonhypochondriacs, are eating right and exercising these days because they want nothing to do with our health-care system, which is looked down upon by people in countries where they ride to work on goats.

If you become quite ill, your first dealings with the U.S. health-care system may well involve the emergency room. This is a place where hundreds of sick, injured, angry, bleeding, vomiting, retching, heaving, shaking, diarrheal, choking people gather to fill out huge amounts of paperwork. Eventually, after several days, the lucky ones get to see a doctor. Or, occasionally, not even a doctor but a resident. A resident is a person who has expressed interest in one day becoming a doctor but who, for the present, may know as much about medicine as a doughnut shop clerk.

While he's called "Doctor," technically a resident is still a student. As a guy who refuses to save ten bucks by letting a student barber cut my hair, needless to say, if I'm seriously ill, I want nothing to do with a resident.

If you don't pass away before you get to see a doctor or resident in the ER, then you may be admitted to the hospital. Men hate hospitals for many of the same reasons they dislike doctors—lack of control, feelings of helplessness. Also, men are forced to don a hospital gown, which is the second least flattering garment ever invented, right behind the bowling shoe.

Once you're in the hospital, be very careful what you request, as everything is overpriced and expensive. The hospital is essentially Starbucks with sick people. Always err on the side of caution when asking for things. If your head hurts in the hospital, suck it up, because a few aspirin can cost you a tidy sum. Before the nurses or doctors give you any medicine, oxygen, tubes, catheters, and so forth, always ask, "How much does that cost?" to avoid surprises. Then, before they administer such treatments, try to barter with them to get the price down.

When in the hospital, you'll frequently be awakened so groups of "students" can stare at you. This is just another way hospitals have of torturing and degrading patients. This is allowed to happen in no other venue.*

Once you get out of the hospital, the fun really begins. If you have health insurance, you will soon begin receiving forms in the mail explaining that the tests and exams you had were not covered. If you don't have health insurance, you're still sitting in the ER waiting to see a doctor.

Under your health-insurance plan, you probably have something called a deductible that almost always is equal to the amount of your bill. For example, if your deductible is $1,000, your bill will usually

* If you have an HMO, these "students" may be from the barber college down the street.

be $1,001.13, so you pay $1,000 and the insurance company covers a buck thirteen.

Not having health insurance is common. Of Americans who apply for private health insurance, 89 percent are turned down. Which means if you live in, say, St. Louis, and you get sick, the closest affordable place to go for treatment is Montreal.

Men hate getting sick for many reasons, not the least of which is all the red tape involved. Assuming you have health insurance, you must know whether you've got a PPO, HMO, IPA, and, ideally, a CPA. Each pays a different percentage of medical claims, but it's impossible to determine what that percentage is until the bill arrives.

Actually, if you have the choice of being treated for a serious medical malady by either an HMO (health-maintenance organization) or a CPA (certified public accountant), always choose the accountant.

The good news is that our health-care system can serve as a motivational tool. What better reason to take good care of yourself than the U.S. health-care system? Dealing with it can kill you.

Where'd You Get Your Degree?

Our health-care system is such a mess, and Americans are so desperate to look young and feel good at modest cost, that people sometimes seek the services of physicians with questionable credentials who will perform medical procedures at bargain-basement rates. The reason these physicians can afford to provide cut-rate prices is a minor technicality: THEY'RE NOT REALLY DOCTORS. Across this great nation, unlicensed, discount physicians are performing procedures in the privacy of their own homes. Some of the patients frequenting these fake doctors are aware they're seeing unlicensed phonies, while other patients are duped.

The spiraling cost of health care has also led folks to seek the services of unlicensed general physicians for routine physical exams. A man posing as a doctor in Massachusetts was recently busted for allegedly performing liposuctions and administering Botox in his basement. People grew suspicious that he wasn't an actual doctor when they learned he didn't play golf and his handwriting was legible. They also noticed that the examination room tended to be damp in wintertime.

This kind of disturbing story seems to be popping up in the

news with increasing frequency. Here are a few tip-offs that your doctor may be a fraud.

- The eye chart on the office wall reads: S U C K E R.

- If you look closely at his diploma, you can see where the words *traffic school* have been erased.

- He mentions that he bought his stethoscope from a Gypsy.

- When checking a mole on your back, he shouts, "Ohhhh, icky poo!"

- He gets a second opinion from a guy on his bowling team named Clem.

- He works for an HMO.

- He tells you to turn around and bend over, then removes his fee from your wallet.

- His diagnostic methods involve using a divining rod.

- At any point during the examination, he gives you a wedgie.

- He advises you to "smoke two Marlboros and call me in the morning."

- His "lab" looks disturbingly like a carport.

- You sit in the waiting room for less than an hour and a half.

- The waiting room contains a magazine published this decade.

- The nurse is chewing tobacco.

- The doctor is on Rollerblades.

- To put you under before surgery, he turns on PBS.

These phony physicians must be stopped. Men are already scared enough of real doctors without having to worry about the fakes.

Dr. Bruce

Americans are so hungry for information on how to stay young and healthy, more and more people are turning to a subspecies of physician called "TV doctors." TV doctors are the cockroaches of the medical profession. Despite this, they're addressed by the television anchor with a deference usually reserved only for the pope and the inventor of Doppler radar. The TV doctors always go by just their first names (to avoid lawsuits). They answer to monikers like "Dr. Bruce," "Dr. Bob," "Dr. Karen," and "Doc Ed." Doc Ed always sounds like a horse to me.

These "doctors," often using incredible hyperbole, convince people they're going to get sick—or that they're sick already. Sadly, if you're a man, there's a good chance you rely on TV doctors for the bulk of your health knowledge.

I'll be sitting back in my recliner after a hard day's work writing jokes, ready to relax for the evening, when on comes Dr. Tim or Dr. Wally to tell me the "nine warning signs of mule fever." By the time the TV doctor reaches number six, I'm convinced I have mule fever. I run to the bedroom screaming at my wife, "I have mule fever!" (Never mind that only six cases of mule fever have been documented, and they all occurred in Borneo in the early nineteenth century and didn't infect people, only mules.) "Dr.

Wally on Channel 7 listed the symptoms, and I have every one!" (I usually stop my rant when my wife recommences snoring.)

By the time the doctor reaches symptom number eight, I'm picking up the phone to make funeral arrangements.

And the warning signs are always the same, no matter what malady the TV doctor is talking about. "Fever, sore throat, fatigue," and so on, and so forth. You know 'em by heart. As Dr. Wally or Dr. Tim or Dr. Habib stares into the camera with conviction and predicts that mule fever will become this week's pandemic and will wipe out one-third of the viewing audience, we feel like running into the street and rioting.

If you're ever tempted to take the advice of a TV doctor, just remember that television is the medium that brings us such worthwhile material as *The Bachelor, Deal or No Deal,* and *My Big Fat Obnoxious Fiancé.* Life is too short and our health too precarious to put in the hands of anyone on TV.

The World's Oldest People

When I worked at *The Tonight Show,* I wrote a joke for Jay Leno that went something like this: "Sad news: the world's oldest man has passed away at age 118. What is it about these 'world's oldest people'? It seems every other month another one dies. It's almost like the title is cursed."

I think we're obsessed with the world's oldest person because it makes the rest of us feel young. "Look here—a woman in Togo lived to be 120! I'm sixty-four, barely middle-aged!"

Instead of being cursed, the world's oldest people seem to be a fortunate lot: inevitably, when one does die, the newspaper obituary will list the world's oldest person's keys to longevity. These might include a steady diet of pork rinds, chocolate cake, beef jerky, cigars, and mayonnaise; hobbies like bungee jumping, body surfing, cliff diving, and, occasionally, alligator wrestling. Apparently the way to live to a ripe old age is to break every health and safety rule in the book.

It's always a joyous event when a man or woman turns, say, 115. They're usually pictured in the paper at their birthday parties, which, one would hope, weren't surprise parties.

The encouraging thing is that the ages of these world's oldest people seems to be creeping up. I attribute these longer lives to the fact that people are staying active longer. Senior citizens keep busy with activities like gardening, bridge, exercise, and playing guitar for the Rolling Stones.

The oldest human who ever lived was a woman in France named Jean Marie Clement, who lived to be 122. She lived so long, she witnessed more than two thousand French military surrenders.

I wouldn't want to live to be the world's oldest person. Talk about stress. There's always some young punk coming up who'd like to take your title.

Supplements: Modern-Day
Pet Rocks?

Americans spend more than $23 billion a year on supplements and vitamins. Do these things do any good?

Many men turn to supplements, even exotic supplements such as Left Rhino Kidney, as a means of staying young. This method appeals to men because it's much easier than attempting to eat a balanced diet.

Increasingly, men are taking more pills, drinks, and elixirs that fall under the heading of "supplements." We're bombarded with stories and articles on the nutritional benefits of vitamins A, B, C, D, and E.

American men also take pills and powders with weird names that are basically just gibberish buzz names. I took folic acid every morning for two years. What is folic acid? I couldn't tell you. What is it supposed to do? No idea. Did I feel better while I was taking folic acid? No. I did feel a little lighter, but all the weight I lost was in my wallet.

Recently, testosterone patches were all the rage for guys. That's because by the time he reaches age seventy, the average man is producing as much testosterone as a Barbie doll. Now we've learned that according to a recent study, testosterone patches don't do much of anything except possibly give a man acne. Which is one way to look younger.

I also took vitamin E supplements for years after reading that vitamin E can help prevent coronary artery disease. Then I read a newspaper article stating that not only doesn't vitamin E prevent coronary artery disease, it may in fact increase your chances of having a heart attack. I was so upset I developed chest pains.

For a while, Americans were hooked on a supplement called DHEA, which was supposed to help us live longer, lose weight, gain weight, and prevent cancer, heart disease, Alzheimer's disease, and colds. This supplement was also rumored to be capable of achieving peace in the Middle East and could probably win on *Dancing with the Stars.*

Here's the bizarre thing: nobody really knows what DHEA is. We're taking this stuff by the truckload, yet we know as much about its composition as we know about what's in a McNugget. The closest we come to defining DHEA is to say it's a cousin to testosterone and estrogen. DHEA has also been dubbed the "superhormone" and the "Fountain of Youth hormone" on the prestigious Internet, an information delivery system approximately half as reliable as *Weekly World News.*

A while back, we were also excited about melatonin, a supplement that could both help you fall asleep and help you stay alert.

As of this writing, men are chomping down on garlic supplements, the new flavor of the week as supplements go. Consuming mass quantities of garlic supposedly helps a person live longer—unless you die of loneliness around age forty-five.

What can we learn from the popularity of supplements? That just as Dorothy, the Tin Man, the Scarecrow, and the Cowardly Lion put all their faith and hope in the Wizard of Oz, so we're all desperate for something that solves our problems. But unlike the Wizard, some of these supplements and vitamins are actually beneficial, especially when our diets lack basically everything except trans fats, hydrogenated oil, and frosting.

Appearance

Vanity, Thy Name Is Ralph

Men usually don't notice wrinkles. We're noticing them more now than in the past, but that's not saying much. Some men are getting face-lifts and Botox and Restylane injections, but most of us don't particularly care about wrinkles. Instead, as we age, we focus on things like our expanding stomachs and our diminished ability to perform athletically.

As far as appearance goes, we're bothered more than anything by our receding hairlines and the bald spot that's growing faster than the population of China. We've been oblivious to the fact that as we aged, the crevices in the middle of our foreheads were growing big enough to envelop a hang glider. But if you believe the articles and TV magazine shows, all this is changing. To try to stay young, more and more people, including men, are injecting all sorts of exotic substances into their faces to reduce or eliminate wrinkles.

I don't do much for my skin, but I do use a daily sunscreen.

As pale as I am (my nickname in college was "Casper," and not because I was friendly), I should have an SPF of around seven thousand. I should go outdoors in daylight hours only during total eclipses.

Men and women are inherently different when it comes to how they feel about their appearance. A man can be seventy-five years old, five feet eight, 350 pounds, with a nose that resembles the Washington Monument (if the Washington Monument had massive amounts of hair growing out of it), and still dance in front of the mirror before his morning shower with his belly fat bouncing from one bathroom wall to the other till it gets stuck in the shower curtain, while holding a toothbrush as a microphone and singing "Da Ya Think I'm Sexy?"

On the other hand, a woman can be a six-foot, 112-pound supermodel, but if she gets one tiny blemish, it's, "Ahhhh, I'm so fat and ugly!"

Most men believe they're appealing to women regardless of how hideous their actual appearance. And thinking we're attractive to the opposite sex doesn't diminish much as we age. Have you seen those gentlemen on the news who are so obese that emergency workers have to cut holes in the walls of their house to get them to a doctor because they won't fit through the door? I'd wager these gentlemen, if they could've fit through the door, would have gone to the beach in a Speedo and imagined that the nineteen-year-old female lifeguard was "checking me out."

Appearance

A while back I saw a morbidly obese guy on the news. Firefighters had to cut him out of his house and then extricate him from the clothes that had been stuck to his body for four years. When they carried him out on a gurney, part of the sofa he'd been lying on for seven years sticking to his torso, he probably checked his reflection in the neighbor's window and, with typical male ego, thought: *Hey, I look good.*

Robert Earl Hughes, for several decades, held the record for being the heaviest human ever. According to *Guinness World Records,* he tipped the scales at a robust 1,069 pounds and had to be buried in a coffin the size of a piano case. If you asked Hughes, he probably would have rated his looks "above average."

Men usually think themselves fairly handsome. That's why we secretly primp in the mirror. If the fire department is about to cut through a wall to rescue our eight-hundred-pound selves, we want to look our best.

Gimme a Head With Hair

One ominous sign of male aging: your friend gets a bad toupee. Hair is a sign of youth and vitality almost as important to a man's sense of well-being as the size of his TV screen or how much he paid for his lawn mower. Men subconsciously equate hair with virility, and losing it is worrisome, so trying to hide that fact is understandable. Still, a bad toupee only draws more attention to a man's hair-challenged plight. There's no easy way to tell a friend it looks like he has a dead ocelot tied to his head. It's much easier to tell a friend his wife is leaving him.

A man usually realizes he needs a toupee when he no longer has enough hair to execute a bad comb-over and must resort to trying to comb the living-room curtains over his bald spot, which almost never looks natural.

Getting a toupee is the next step for a man desperate to hold on to his youth. Some toupees look good. The other 99.9 percent are bad. Of course, there's a technical term for those with really bad toupees. That term is *televangelist.*

The frightening thing about balding is that you usually don't realize your hair is disappearing until you look like Mr. Clean. One harbinger you may be getting there is if you look down during your morning shower, and the drain resembles Cousin Itt from *The Addams Family.* Or you wake up in the morning and mistake your pillow for Ed Asner's back. Or when a camera crew from *20/20* shows up in your driveway tracking Sasquatch.

You can find some over-the-counter fixes for balding, but most of the time they don't cure the affliction, but just keep it from progressing. Such products include Rogaine and Propecia. These are for men who want to stay the course. You may not look good now; you just don't want to look any worse . . . which is kind of depressing.

The "balding industry" is a huge one. Tons of books, videos, infomercials, and board games (okay, I made up the board games) are aimed squarely at the balding man. The Yellow Pages are chock full of ads for doctors who perform hair transplants, with testimonials from their overly hirsute patients who resemble video images from a few years ago of Bigfoot coming out of the woods.

The one guy I knew who underwent a hair transplant was not exactly satisfied. Postsurgery he resembled half a Chia Head, with hair growing prodigiously on just one side of his scalp. I advised him to pay only half the bill.

What really amuses me is that all the doctors in the ads who perform hair transplants have too much hair. Elderly gents shouldn't have such huge amounts of hair. Picture the Crypt Keeper with Donny Osmond hair. It's out of proportion.

As men lose hair, we tend to wear ball caps. Groups of guys in their fifties typically look like groups of twelve-year-olds—both have the mandatory ball caps securely in place. But unlike twelve-year-olds, the hair-loss guys wear their caps with the bills facing front.

The top of a man's head is one place about which he's a bit vain. A guy can be overweight, covered with pockmarks, and have three-day-old cheese stuck in his beard, and he's fine with it all. In fact, he'll pride himself on his work ethic if he thinks to pluck some of the cheese and eat it for lunch while sitting at his desk. Sometimes he'll even rub crackers through his beard to spread cheese on them. And he's content. That is, until he finds a single hair on his comb. At this his reaction is akin to that of a guy who discovers a water moccasin in the toilet while seated.

"I'm going bald!" the man will yell through the three-day-old cheese in his whiskers. "I found a hair on my comb. Call 911!"

Of course, 911 operators do not respond to these calls. They just chuckle knowingly and hang up.

Some men eventually accept their receding hairlines. The other 70 percent seek a cure for baldness to their dying day. It's as if men take all the concerns you'd think they would have—getting fat, growing ears as large as an elephant's, hair protruding from their nostrils so their sniffers look like a rain forest—ignore them all and pour all their vanity into a single concern: not going bald.

Gee, Your Head Looks Terrific

As a man ages, if his hair isn't falling out in clumps the size of birds' nests, it's probably turning gray. My hair began turning gray in my early thirties, approximately two days after my acne cleared up. So I had forty-eight good hours, then—poof—another problem.

Whether for vanity or to better compete in the workplace by looking younger, more men than ever are coloring their gray hair. If you choose to do this, you have two options: use an over-the-counter product or go to a salon.

If you use an over-the-counter product, you risk walking around with hair the color of Cheetos. Then people will laugh at you and call you "Cheeto Head." Small children will point at you in public and run crying into their mothers' arms. Women will recoil in disgust. You'll likely become a recluse—a hermit, even—shunned by society, growing old alone: a solitary, broken man. This is still better than going to a salon to have your hair colored.

As one who has undergone hair coloring in a salon, let me walk you through the process before you decide whether you're willing to pay the price for young hair.

Right off the top, I'd like to say I'd rather have a root canal done by a blind auto mechanic using a garden hoe than have my hair colored in a salon. I last had my hair colored in a salon five years ago, and I'm just now recovering from post-traumatic stress disorder.

When you first enter the salon, your imagination runs wild. You presume that all heads are turning toward you and women are thinking, *A man? Getting his hair done here? How incredibly strange.* Only you're not just imagining this: that's exactly what they're thinking.

After checking in at the front desk (ideally, under an assumed name: I favor "Skip Snodgrass" and "Harry Palate"), you walk into a little closet and take one from a row of smocks. This was the most awkward I'd felt selecting a garment since fifth grade, when my grandmother took me shopping for an athletic supporter.

After donning a smock, you'll enter the hair-coloring area of the salon. This is every bit as emasculating as walking into the examination room of a gynecologist's office. Be very careful, as the level of estrogen in this area often reaches toxic levels. You'll then sit down amid a row of women, who are also getting their hair dyed. Soon you'll be more uncomfortable than you've been in your entire life. You won't feel welcome in the least. Judging by the stares of the women in this chic salon, you'd think you were a junkyard dog someone dragged in to be groomed.

To make matters worse, the women on either side of you will invariably be in the middle of a five-hour discussion about some type of "female trouble."

Appearance

After leaving you squirming for an hour or so listening to these conversations, the hair-coloring technician will approach and ask if she can get you anything. I usually try to compensate by asking for some power tools and a shot put, which the salon tech is never able to provide. Then this person begins the hair-coloring procedure. He or she will cover your hair with something like aluminum foil, then place your head under a large machine. The technical name for this apparatus is "the hair-coloring machine." The purpose of the foil is to make you look like an even bigger idiot. You'll resemble one of those guys you see on the news claiming he was taken hostage by aliens.

Sitting under the hair-coloring machine with your head wrapped in foil in the midst of a group of women getting their nails and hair done is the most effeminate thing a man can do.

Eventually the hair-coloring person returns and takes your noggin out of the machine. She removes the foil, examines your head for burn marks, and, assuming she doesn't find any, sends you to the front desk, where you pay as much to color your thinning hair as Earl Scheib would charge to paint your Ford Excursion.

So why do large numbers of men put themselves through this agonizing ordeal? Because more than ever, the emphasis in our society is on youth. And if society dictates that men who otherwise look like death warmed over shall have the same hue of hair they had in fourth grade, then so be it.

Botox for Men

When men aren't coloring their hair, these days they may be getting Botox. Physicians estimate that 12 percent of all Botox injections are given to men. As I said before, most men don't notice wrinkles. But a few do, and their numbers are increasing. In the name of research for this book, and because I can deduct it on my taxes if I write about it, I decided to try Botox just once.

I probably needed Botox anyway. Since I was young, I've had forehead creases that look like tributaries of the Grand Canyon. I once woke from a nap to find two guys spelunking just above my nose. I could carry my wallet in my forehead. When I was growing up during the Cold War, my forehead was designated the neighborhood bomb shelter. If that little girl who fell down the well in Texas had fallen into the crease in my forehead, they might never have rescued her.

After arriving at the plastic surgeon's office, I sat in the waiting room surrounded by a phalanx of middle-aged women who gave me the same kind of looks they'd give their ex-husbands' divorce attorneys. To kill time I tried to guess why each woman was visiting a plastic surgeon. Woman A was likely there for crow's-feet, woman B for a face-lift, and woman C for rhinoplasty. Reasoning that Los Angeles has experienced enough civil unrest, I kept my opinions to myself.

After a short time, a nurse led me into the examination/treatment room, where I met the nice plastic surgeon. I drilled him and learned that those heavy frown lines on my forehead are called "glabellar creases." I also learned that he's seeing more and more men for Botox injections, including many local newscasters. (It's easy to spot the anchor guys who've had Botox. When some dramatic, newsworthy event happens in the world, like Britney Spears leaving a coffee shop with her baby tied to the luggage rack,* they can't raise their eyebrows.) The other men who get Botox tend to be actors, executives, or "metrosexual" types. The doctor said he doesn't administer Botox to many construction workers or longshoremen.

The doctor asked if I was nervous. Because he was about to shoot botulinum toxin, a virulent poison that causes botulism, into my face, I admitted that yes, I felt slight trepidation.

The actual Botox shot was fast and fairly painless. After paying six hundred dollars and learning it would take about a week for the Botox to completely kick in, I was off, nodding knowingly to the woman still waiting for her crow's-feet treatment.

Each day for the next week, I looked in the mirror to check my progress. The crease on my forehead gradually diminished

* This didn't really happen . . . yet.

until, after six days, although it was still there, it wasn't nearly as prominent. Instead of a tributary of the Grand Canyon, the wrinkles looked more like rain gutters. So now I walk around with vertical rain gutters on my forehead. I also noticed one tiny, trivial, inconsequential side effect: the top one-third of my face was completely paralyzed. I couldn't lift my eyebrows to save my life. It was impossible for me to register surprise, happiness, or excitement. I looked like Mr. Spock. Granted, a young Mr. Spock. Which is what it's all about.

Our Aging Presidents

One guy too busy to worry about getting older is the president of the United States. There's always been tremendous attention given to the rate the president, whomever it happens to be at the time, is aging. Especially if he's aging badly. Which is actually a good thing. I want a president who looks ten years older six weeks after taking office. If a president looks too good, he's not worrying enough about the world we live in. I never want to hear my president referred to as "America's oldest teenager." A man should not age gracefully in that job.

That's why, in diametrical opposition to most historians, I feel our finest president ever—far superior to Washington, Jefferson, Lincoln, Roosevelt, et al.—was Jimmy Carter. Carter was a man who obviously stayed up late fretting about things. Carter is lauded for his work with Habitat for Humanity, building houses for the homeless, winning a Nobel Peace Prize, and monitoring elections in hundreds of foreign countries all ending in "istan." He's also remembered as the president who aged so quickly in office that he sometimes developed new wrinkles during press conferences. During one memorable State of the Union address, Carter developed five new age spots and his jowls dropped three inches. During one G7 meeting, his hair went from dark brown to white-gray. Sometimes, during stressful news conferences, liver spots were observed to multiply on Carter's face while hair sprouted visibly from his ears and nose.

Say what you wish about Carter, he cared about the job. The fact that Carter went from bearing a slight resemblance to a *Happy Days*-era Ron Howard at the beginning of his term, to four years later bearing a striking similarity to Buddy Ebsen, proves it.

Calf Implants

Jimmy Carter never resorted to silly plastic surgery. But some men do. A few years ago someone conducted a survey on the most popular plastic surgeries for men. You might guess that the most common would be a nose job. Or maybe a chin tuck or jowl-lift. Or an ego reduction. But no, the most common plastic surgery for men was a calf implant, whereby an artificial device is inserted into the calf, making it appear larger. Thousands of these surgeries are performed every year.

This study proves that some men are certifiably insane. It also proves that some men have absolutely no concept of what it takes to be attractive to women. Men ignore important personal aspects they could improve to good effect: having a good complexion, a nice smile, a well-developed personality, and a keen intellect. Instead, they focus on developing their calves—and not even the natural way.

I would never have a calf implant, even though, as a skinny guy, both of my calves combined when I was growing up were slightly thinner than a piece of dental floss. My lower extremities look like exclamation marks with shoes. But I learned to live with this affliction by always wearing long pants. Between the ages of nine and seventeen, I never removed my pants except for my biannual shower.

I think the fact that many men feel the key to happiness is spending thousands of dollars to inflate the size of their calves is also a sign that society is becoming phenomenally shallow. I'm in good position to gauge this trend, as I live in Los Angeles, which is to shallowness what Idaho is to potatoes, Paris to amour, and Washington, D.C., to buffoonery. L.A. is a city where the typical person's life goal is to attain inner happiness and spiritual fulfillment by appearing on *Deal or No Deal.* In L.A. the typical man is slightly more vain than the average contestant in America's Junior Miss pageant.

In Los Angeles our other life goal often is simply looking good. And we're willing to pay the price—even if that price is being detained for five hours at the airport trying to convince the Department of Homeland Security that the reason we keep setting off the metal detector is that there's a steel plate in our calf.

Could men put their resources to better use than calf implants? Sure. Try explaining to little Billy someday that he can't go to college because Dad blew seven thousand dollars when Billy was nine so Dad could have bigger calves.

Dressing to Please

Thanks to the styles of today, a middle-aged guy can feel comfortable showing off his enhanced calves by wearing skateboarding shorts.

One of the ways men try to retain their youth is by dressing as if they're, say, forty years younger than they actually are. When it comes to clothes, eighty is the new thirty. Baby boomers are the first generation to continue to wear the same type of clothes they wore in college into their sixties. This is the first generation of couples who—the husbands sporting Abercrombie & Fitch sweatshirts and baggy Diesel jeans, the wives in bicycle shorts and blouses from Forever 21—pony up to the counter at Sizzler and ask for the senior discount.

Twenty years ago people dressed their age. When men reached middle age, they put away the jeans and donned bright Bermuda shorts, suspenders, and white high-top shoes. Sure, they looked like color-blind carnival barkers or overweight, hideously unattractive male ice dancers, but we knew they were dads. Now middle-aged men resemble high school freshmen with disease that causes premature aging. Apparently the reasoning is, "If we can't turn back the clock, we can at least fake that we've turned back the clock."

The other day at the mall, I saw a gentleman who looked around eighty wearing a pair of tight blue jeans, a muscle shirt, and running shoes. I'm not sure where he was going to be running, but at the speed he was crossing the mall (estimated time to get from the food court to Sears: four and a half days), he wasn't going to be running far.

And the frightening thing is, people seem to be dressing younger every year. At the rate we're going, we'll soon see elderly folks sporting baggy jeans, backward ball caps, and belly shirts. Down the road, guys in their nineties will be wearing bonnets while carrying pacifiers and blankets.

If this makes people feel better or feel younger, there's nothing wrong with that. We may look ridiculous, but at least we feel young.

Trends

Da Do Ron Ron

The middle-aged guy of today doesn't have to stop with dressing as if he is in high school; he can also listen to the same music he did in high school. This is why I urge young people to be selective about what music they illegally download on the Internet. The type of music a man listens to in adolescence is often the same music he will groove to for his entire life, no matter how embarrassing and inappropriate. I believe this is partly psychological, as middle-aged men subconsciously try to regain their youth by jamming to Jan and Dean, the Beach Boys, and Chuck Berry well into their sixties and seventies.

I hope I'm wrong on the above hypothesis, as this scenario leads to a scary possibility for the future: men in their seventies and eighties listening to rap. Like cars that can fly, I probably won't live to see this come to fruition, and I'm glad. It's bad enough now, as baby boomers head into their sixties bobbing their heads to Led Zeppelin and Jimi Hendrix on their iPods.

the **Male Team**

Bill Clinton's inauguration in 1993 was a perfect example of folks' not letting go of the music they listened to in their younger days. Remember that inaugural celebration? You had a bunch of well-to-do men and women grooving to the sounds of Fleetwood Mac, a group that was big in the seventies. The inauguration would have been truly embarrassing if the Clintons had been fans of, say, the Archies.

Clinton was being touted as a bright new face on the national political scene, yet his inaugural ball looked like a tea dance for geeky boomers.

So next time you hear your kid listening to loud music in his room, know that it's even worse than you imagine. Not only is he neglecting his homework for hip-hop, but one day he'll be eighty years old and, quite conceivably, listening to hip-hop. Now *that's* frightening.

Still, if listening to thirty-year-old music helps us to feel young, it's probably a good thing. If I close myself in my room with my old record player and Freddy Fender and Foghat (I have eclectic taste) vinyl records, please leave me alone. Something will be going on that transcends music.

Th-th-that's All, Folks!

Not only do we listen to the music of our adolescence as we age, but many baby boomers still enjoy spending a quiet evening out watching cartoons. The reason Hollywood studios keep pumping out one animated feature after another is partly that audiences are starved for family entertainment. I believe this is a backlash from all the gratuitous sex and violence in films. Folks are sick of it. But another reason studios release so many animated films is that we may be the first group of people to continue being amused by animated frogs, walruses, and turtles well into our golden years.

Last year I took my nephews to see an animated feature called *Barnyard*. The film was targeted at viewers from four to fourteen. However, I noticed a number of older couples and several unaccompanied men in the theater. Laughing. At animated cows saying, "It's time for bed, Grover. I think I'll put on my muumuu." (Not an actual quote from the movie. The actual dialogue was even stupider.) I think these baby boomers were in that theater applauding for animated livestock because it made them feel young.

And why shouldn't it? There's nothing wrong with paying ten

bucks to watch a two-hour cartoon. It's probably better for adults to watch these animated features than for kids to watch them. What are we trying to teach youngsters? We could be raising a generation that believes frogs fly, hedgehogs yodel, and moose do the waltz! Everyone knows moose can only tango.

Then again, perhaps this is why Social Security is going broke and we're falling behind China. Our country is run by a generation of sixty-somethings who still watch cartoons.

Another Reason to Take Care of Yourself: Drive-Through Mortuaries

A while back, in the city of Los Angeles, the world's first drive-through mortuary opened. I can't think of better incentive for taking care of yourself and living to a ripe old age.

What can be more degrading than lying in an open coffin as a group of your relatives and friends (and tourists who got lost looking for the freeway) pass by and toss flowers (probably plastic) from their vehicles? That's telling—when your loved ones don't miss you enough to get out of their Land Rovers.

I don't want a lot at my funeral. A decent casket and a simple eulogy will suffice. Maybe mention the time I bowled a two hundred game or was nearly selected captain of the safety patrol in sixth grade. But please—*get out of your cars.*

Supposedly this drive-through mortuary could be a trend of the future and spread from L.A. to places where normal people live. Which is yet another reason to worry about getting older.

I think the worst thing about a drive-through funeral is that this lends itself to doing other activities while viewing the departed. I've been having recurrent nightmares of my loved ones eating, bobbing their heads in rhythm to the car CD player, and talking on their cell phones as they gaze at my casket. I usually wake up in a cold sweat.

Let's hope this trend stops here. I don't want my funeral to be a drive-by. And I can't think of anything more tasteless than having mourners hit up the family of the dearly departed for gas money.

Dad or Granddad?

Some men try to hang on to their youth by becoming fathers—increasingly, first-time fathers at more advanced ages. Just look at all the older men who've fathered children the past few years—David Letterman, Tony Randall,* Hugh Hefner, actor Anthony Quinn,† and Donald Trump. Media mogul Rupert Murdoch's wife gave birth when he was seventy. The reason for this trend could be that men genuinely want to reproduce and create a living, breathing being and leave a lasting legacy. Or they want to prove their virility and have a child for more vain reasons. I think the names Trump and Murdoch lend support to this theory.

It actually makes sense for men to become fathers, even first-time fathers, after age sixty. Think of the positives:

- Dad and Baby go into diapers at the same time.

- Baby gets his teeth the same time Daddy loses his.

- Dad and Baby can keep each other company the twenty-five times per night they get up.

* Fathered his first child at age seventy-seven.
† Fathered enough children at an advanced age to populate Dayton, Ohio.

- Mom can cut Baby's food into little pieces at the same time she cuts Dad's food into little pieces.

- Dad and Baby are both dazzled by the same bright objects.

Now it's more confusing than ever when you see a small baby with an elderly man. It used to be you were safe in saying, "Ah, that's a cute grandchild." Now you can't be certain of the relationship between any man and baby. So when you see a seventy-year-old man with a tyke, you have to say something politically correct, and stupid, like, "What a lovely child."

I miss the old days, when you just had to be concerned about mistaking a little boy for a girl or vice versa. I recently hit the daily double when I said to a guy at a public swimming pool, "You have a cute granddaughter"—and he explained that the child in question was, in fact, his son. Go figure.

Even so, older guys fathering children probably makes sense. If you decide to wait till the typical guy is mature enough to have a kid, eighty to eighty-five sounds about right.

The Polar Bear Club

When older men aren't fathering children, they often can be found diving into freezing bodies of water. I look forward to every New Year's Day, but not because it's an opportunity to begin anew. Not because it's a day to share with family and friends. Not because there are 139 football games on TV. I look forward to New Year's Day because of an amusing group called the Polar Bear Club—mostly older folks who try to convince themselves they're still young by disrobing and running into bodies of ice-cold water.

Some of these "polar bears" are getting up in age. The first time I saw members of the Polar Bear Club running into freezing water, I thought our Supreme Court justices had finally dropped their robes and gone off the deep end.

If you've never seen the Polar Bear Club in action, picture an episode of *The Golden Girls* in which the girls go ice fishing and fall through the ice.

Members of the Polar Bear Club don't just stick a toe in the water. These people venture out from snow-packed "beaches" and submerge themselves! They revel in it.

At one time only one Polar Bear Club existed, and one group of people who made a mad dash into freezing water on New

Year's Day. But Polar Bear Clubs spread around the world, not unlike bird flu, and are now seen in many locations.

Initially I thought the Polar Bear Club got its name because its members have half the IQ of your average polar bear. But then I realized what an invigorating thing it must be to run into an icy ocean. Belonging to the Polar Bear Club is a great way to feel young and alive—provided it doesn't kill you.

I Can't Drive Fifty-five
After I Turn Fifty-five

The stereotype is that men buy sports cars in an attempt to hold on to their youth and attractiveness. In many cases this stereotype happens to be true.

The velocity of a middle-aged man's car is frequently in direct proportion to the speed at which he is losing hair. What is it, exactly, that makes a man want ten additional horsepower for every one hundred hair follicles he loses? Perhaps it's because when men lose something in one area, we try to compensate by gaining in another area. That's why, many times, guys who don't have large incomes work out and get big muscles. And why men who aren't overly intelligent have the shiniest shoes. And why men under five feet seven often act as if they're fourteen feet tall.

The more a man is balding, the more he wants a sports car. That's why when you visit the showroom of a Porsche or Corvette dealership, you sometimes have to wade through chest-deep shed hair follicles. It might actually be possible to drown in follicles at a Porsche dealership.

Women readers may be asking, "Why don't men compensate for their receding hairlines and other age-related shortcomings by developing their minds, their sense of humor, their personality, and their compassion?" To that I would reply, "Do you even know any men, lady?!" What a waste of time, to develop all those things, when that cherry-red Mustang comes with a fifteen-hundred-dollar rebate!

Try this game. Every time you spot a nice sports car on the street, take note and count how often the driver is a balding man. Then look for more conservative sedans on the road and count how often the driver is a balding male. Based on my exhaustive ten-year study, I find that a staggering 35 percent of people who drive nice sports cars are balding males. Thirty-five percent. Far larger than the percentage of balding men driving conservative, nonsporty vehicles.

Defying all logic, an incredibly large percentage of convertible drivers are balding males. When your hair is falling out, do you really need the additional embarrassment of creating a safety hazard on the interstate by having it become airborne? Do you someday want to pick up a newspaper and read the following report? "Jonas Beckal was in fair condition at a local hospital after his car went off the road into a ravine. The vehicle spun out of control after a large clump of hair from a balding man, identified as Edward R. Finkel, 123 East Hampton Road, driving a Mustang convertible, flew off and completely covered the windshield of the car behind him. Prosecutors are considering filing charges. It is believed that Finkel was in the throes of a midlife crisis."

So be aware that there's a definite downside to balding men driving some sports cars.

Overall, what do my studies prove? Mostly that I have far too much time on my hands. But they also offer conclusive proof that men think bald is beautiful only when bald is behind the wheel of a Testarossa.

Staying in School—Forever

A number of older, balding guys are driving their sports cars to school. Increasingly, college campuses are populated with book-bag-carting folks who look as if they're going to school on the GI Bill for their service in World War II. These older students are most likely to major in history. That way, if a professor tries to correct their answers about something that happened, say, during the Eisenhower administration or the Bay of Pigs invasion, the older student can say, "Hey—I was there."

Every spring our newspapers and newscasts carry stories about people in their sixties, seventies, eighties, and even nineties who are graduating from high school or college. One paper described an eighty-two-year-old university graduate as a "typical liberal arts major"—which means postgraduation, he moved back in with his parents.

I think it's a wonderful idea for seniors and baby boomers to return to campus. In fact, so many seniors are returning to college that there's talk of establishing a fraternity for the aged. Instead of a traditional frat house, it'll offer assisted living.

The purpose of older people returning to college surely must be so they can recapture their youth. Why else would an octogenarian get a degree? So he can improve his work prospects for the future?

Let seniors return to college. Let them learn and grow and gain life skills. Just don't let them try to tear down the goal posts after football victories.

Everybody's Working
for the Weekend

By the time he gets into his forties, a man usually has a definite game plan for the weekend. And that plan generally involves a recliner, a cool beverage, and a big-screen TV roughly the size of Saturn. That's it. Even men who don't enjoy sports, once they hit forty, love to sit in that recliner, remote in hand, flipping from one channel to another and watching twenty-year-old episodes of *Love Boat* and public access programs featuring people playing seventeenth-century Indian folk music on crude, handmade instruments. When we think that life may be passing us by in the outside world, we smile: that's how we like it. We prefer watching Moroccan lawn bowling on ESPN2 to "life." We prefer watching Australian-rules football to "life." Heck, we'd rather watch a rerun of a 1978 preseason football game on ESPN Classic than deal with "life" on a weekend. "Life" can disappoint you. When you have a remote in your hand and your backside glued to a recliner, you don't need "life." "Life" is for people who don't have cable.

Men spend entire weekends sitting in front of the television to "recharge." In the long run, they believe this will add years to their lives, which they'll undoubtedly use to watch more television in their recliners. Some middle-aged guys I know couldn't be pried out of their recliners on the weekend with the Jaws of Life.

If their house caught fire, the fire department would have to carry out the entire recliner to rescue the napping man.

Or, if the man somehow made it out of the house, he'd run back in—braving the fire and stepping over the comatose family cat—to rescue his recliner. Personally, I'm thinking of moving a recliner under the doorjamb so I can sit safely even in the event of an earthquake.

Last year an entrepreneur, a modern-day Benjamin Franklin/Thomas Edison/Albert Einstein, came up with a recliner featuring a built-in refrigerator. If they let average guys vote for the Pulitzer and Nobel prizes, this guy would win in a landslide. Discovering cold fusion is a fine thing, but a recliner with a built-in fridge? Now that's inspired. I may learn this gentleman's name and vote for him for president. As a result of this ingenious invention, which in a historical sense is every bit as significant as the discovery of electricity or invention of the wheel, men can literally go for years without leaving the house. As a matter of fact, if I can get my hands on one of those recliners, I may never walk outside again. When I die, they can bury me seated on my recliner. It may make for one ridiculous open casket, but at least I'll look comfortable. And I'll have no complaints.

By the way, men spend so much time in recliners that I predict by the year 2100, male babies will actually be born with tiny La-Z-Boys attached to their backsides. They'll never again have to walk to a recliner, making for an even more effortless weekend.

Large-Print Books

Old age is the most unexpected of all
the things that happen to a man.
—Leon Trotsky

Thanks to advances in publishing, guys will soon be able to read large-print books while sitting in our recliners on the weekend. A group of major publishers recently announced a line of large-print edition paperbacks for people over forty. This is an extremely wise business decision, as the market should be tremendous. Estimates say that by the year 2020, 33 percent of Americans will be age sixty-five or older.

The goal of the large-print books is to allow aging baby boomers to read without the assistance of reading glasses. Which is a good idea. Most middle-aged men would rather be seen in support hose than in reading glasses.

Reading glasses are an obvious sign of aging. My former employer, Jay Leno, regularly wears reading glasses in the office that make him look like a cross between Ebenezer Scrooge and a lantern-jawed Grandma Moses. In all the years of doing the program, he never appeared on camera in his reading glasses for fear that viewers would mistake the show for *The Tonight Show with Grandma Moses,* which might scare off the coveted youth demographic.

We need large-print paperback books. That's a good start. Here are a few more suggestions for products as boomers age:

- TVs with extra-loud sound so everybody sounds like Chris Matthews

- Extra-large oat bran so you can find it in your bowl

- Cars with magnifying-glass windshields so aging motorists can read road signs

- Toilets that fold out into beds so a man has a place to sleep during all those nightly visits to the bathroom

Honey, They Shrunk My Brain

Unfortunately, we may not be able to comprehend what we're reading in our large-print books. According to a new study, aging men's brains tend to shrink. That's yet another reason not to be thrilled with getting older. What's to like about a process whereby your nose, ears, feet, and waistline grow, while your brain shrinks?

This study means that by the time he's ninety-five, the average man will be unable to find the television remote even when it's in his hand. By the time we reach sixty, we won't be able to open a road map, let alone read one. Men will get lost trying to find their own kitchens, and they'll refuse to ask for directions.

Combine the shrinking of aging brains with the vast numbers of baby boomers for a truly scary plight. Soon the world will be populated largely with elderly people who don't know what they're doing, as their minuscule brains barely function. These folks will spend their days walking around looking for things they dropped five minutes ago. We'll devote hours to sitting motionless in front of the washing machine wondering how it is that we put two socks into the washer and only one comes out.

Despite all we try to do to maintain our youth, so far there's nothing we can do to compensate for shrinking brains. And here's a sobering thought: that teenage guy outside your house on a skateboard with jeans falling four inches shy of his ankles with the pierced tongue who can't spell *cat** and who thinks New Jersey is a city may one day have a brain that's even smaller than it is now.

That's just the way it is. Let us men continue heading into the future at forty miles per hour with our turn signals blinking. Let us bravely face the future sans Social Security, without savings, and with our brains shriveling. Ah, the golden years.

---

* Also, when he tries to say *cat* with his pierced tongue, it comes out *tat*.

Exercise

No Pain, No Gain

Remember years ago, before the running craze hit this country? Back then, if you saw anyone over twenty running down the street, you'd assume there'd been a purse snatching or a bank robbery. Today it's more than likely the middle-aged person running down the street is jogging.

Baby boomer men feel that if they exercise till they drop, they just might be able to keep old age at bay. That's why the typical gym contains more aging Americans than a Denny's at dusk. So many, in fact, that more and more, the phrase, "I'll spot you," is being replaced with, "I'll liver spot you."

Many of these elderly denizens of the gym are not casual weekend warriors. They take their exercise seriously. And with recent studies indicating that cardio exercise and weight-resistance training can prolong life and stave off maladies such as arthritis, why shouldn't they?

Throughout the country, niche gyms tailored for the over-fifty set are opening so those who aren't quite as limber, fast, or strong as they once were can work out without being intimidated by the four-hundred-pound guy who's lifting a house. These over-fifty niche gyms are targeted at those who don't want to work out in Home Depot–sized gyms filled with loud music and spandex. Which is basically anybody with half a brain.

But perhaps the gyms should market their services to those over, say seventy, because men in their fifties still think they can do the same fitness activities as when they were eighteen. These guys fail to accurately gauge their current strength and sometimes end up in the emergency room with their heads stuck inside a medicine ball.

But that's still better than working out in an over-fifty gym.

The SilverSneakers (sounds better than "Stale Shoes") Fitness Program, exclusively for seniors, has expanded to twelve hundred gyms and YMCAs across the country as people increasingly recognize the direct correlation between exercising and staying young. Older people work out to stay healthy and live longer. Indeed, every male exercise fanatic has a moment of epiphany—usually around age fifty—when he realizes he's no longer working out to look good but rather to stay alive.

Older folks have gotten into exercise to such an extent that many marathons now have age-group awards for participants age eighty and over. Many of these individuals run their race in five or six hours, which is why I've never entered the local marathon. I have a deep-seated fear of showing up on the local sportscast being passed in the homestretch by a guy who looks like the late senator Strom Thurmond in sneakers.

I recently began running for the first time since I was in high school, thirty years ago. My times are almost as good as they were then. The major difference is, instead of five minutes, it takes me a week and a half after my workout to stop sweating.

The Bench Press

Guys wanting to ward off the effects of aging sometimes shun running and cardio exercise and focus instead on building muscle mass. Many men's attempts to stay youthful consist of hitting the gym several nights a week to see how much weight they can bench-press. At best, this is faulty logic. How big a man's chest, arms, and shoulders are has virtually nothing to do with how young he looks. But lots of guys think the secret to looking young is to build a neck thicker than the Manhattan phone book. Ironically, it turns out a neck that size is actually less attractive to women than the Manhattan phone book.

Indeed, occasionally some survey asks women how they feel about muscle-bound men. These studies invariably show that women find huge muscles to be slightly less attractive than a heavy wax buildup in the ears. However, I'm skeptical of these surveys, because according to them, women always say the single most attractive thing about a man is his sense of humor. That's the politically correct thing to say. That's why when pollsters ask people if they plan to vote, most people say yes, leading pollsters to announce that they expect an 85 percent turnout on Election Day. Then Election Day comes and goes, and the actual turnout is closer to 4 percent because people find something better to do than vote, such as watching a special on the "Moths of Nicaragua" on the Home and Garden Network.

So keep pumping away, you muscle-bound dudes. Delude yourself into thinking that big muscles will keep you young. If you're smart, instead of seeing how much weight you can bench-press, you'll modify your workout. Start lifting lighter weights and doing more repetitions—and throw in some exercises to maintain flexibility. These are the things that affect how young you'll look and feel. And then *maybe* you'll be as attractive as earwax.

Presidents: They Love to Run!

President George W. Bush is probably our most fit president ever. At first blush, being named "most fit" of a group that includes Chester Arthur, Rutherford B. Hayes, William Howard Taft, and Grover Cleveland doesn't sound all that impressive. But Mr. Bush was a serious runner well into his fifties, until his knees finally gave out.

Bush routinely ran three miles in around twenty minutes, faster than many trained athletes half his age. And he looked athletic doing so. Most of our presidents have been so unathletic, they've resembled members of the Botswana Olympic Snowboard Team or Rosie O'Donnell trying to play baseball in *A League of Their Own.*

Many of our presidents and candidates in recent years have appeared on television while running, probably because they believe this projects an image of youthful vitality. If our candidates spent half as much time pondering the issues as they do running through the streets during campaigns in ill-fitting short shorts, this country would be a better place. It's completely unnecessary for candidates to run (in the exercise sense) to win our vote. Americans will continue to select our commander in chief in the same way we almost always have—by voting for the taller guy.

But run they do. At the rate we're going, instead of televised debates to choose a president, by the 2020 election we'll just have a footrace down Pennsylvania Avenue.

Why do we choose our political leaders based on who seems the best looking, the tallest, or the one who works out the most or has the best dye job? Instead, we should choose our presidents based on their positions on the important issues facing the world today—like war, the economy, and whether the NFL needs instant replay.

Bill Clinton was another leading presidential jogger. In stark contrast to President Bush's fine form, Clinton resembled an albino Bob's Big Boy waddling down the road in running shorts eight sizes too small.

Jimmy Carter was a runner, too. Better than Clinton but not nearly as good as Bush, Carter often appeared on the news going for long, long daily runs, perhaps to escape work, which must've made the Iranian hostages nervous.

Most of our presidents have exercised.

John F. Kennedy loved to play touch football and swim.

George H. W. Bush enjoyed fly-fishing. The elder Bush also played horseshoes, a rigorous sport in which participants burn up to two calories per hour of activity. Horseshoes is so dull that if Bush had made POWs watch him play, it would've been a breach of the Geneva convention.

Richard Nixon's exercise of choice was bowling, which is perhaps a good enough reason to impeach him.

Presidential candidate John Kerry enjoyed windsurfing. I

think the common man had trouble voting for a president who windsurfs.

Many other presidents played golf, perhaps the most time-consuming "sport." A single round could keep a president occupied for hours, which probably goes a long way toward explaining the messes this country regularly gets into.

But George W. is still our fittest president. These days Bush loves to mountain bike—an activity he hasn't quite mastered, as evidenced by the fact that every few weeks Bush is shown on the evening news hurtling over the bicycle handlebars and through the air like one of the Flying Wallendas before smashing headfirst into a rock and bouncing down an embankment on his Texas ranch. Which probably hasn't helped his confidence rating as leader of the free world.

Still, Mr. Bush bounces right back up because he is in magnificent shape. He sets a great fitness example for the rest of the country. According to the results of the president's last physical exam, his resting pulse rate is around forty-five beats per minute. If he didn't have the most stressful job on the planet, his pulse rate would probably be something like seven beats per minute.

Do I sleep easy at night knowing the president is so relaxed that his pulse is equal to that of a hibernating bear? Not on your life. I'd feel better if he had an ulcer. But at least he's not on TV during the workweek, bowling.

What Do They Want?

The president doesn't only make exercise choices for himself; he employs councils and officials who make recommendations for the entire nation. In my feeble attempts to remain vibrant, healthy, and fit, I try to stay abreast of the latest advances and reports from these councils and officials. What I find most frustrating about trying to maintain healthy habits is that the recommendations of medical authorities constantly change. It used to be that twenty minutes of exercise three times a week was good enough. Then, when the people who decide how much we should exercise realized hardly anybody was doing that, they did the only sensible thing—they upped the time. If we continue ignoring the recommendations, soon we'll be told to exercise nonstop, twenty-four hours a day.

As it stands now, according to the federal guidelines and the President's Council on Physical Fitness and Sports, Americans are strongly encouraged to exercise for thirty minutes every day, which is ridiculous. I know people in their forties and fifties who haven't completed thirty minutes of exercise in their entire lives.

Who has time to exercise for half an hour each day? But fear not: it turns out it's not all that daunting. The half hour of exercise doesn't have to be real exercise. If you look at the government's list of what's considered "exercise," you'll find such physically challenging activities as gardening!

Here's a quick overview of the types of activity the government would likely regard as "exercise."

- Gardening

- Coughing

- Sneezing

- Putting plates into the dishwasher

- Taking plates out of the dishwasher

- Licking cookie dough off your fingers

- Dialing a phone

- Snoring

- Trying to fasten your belt

- Scratching your nose

- Using a Q-tip in your ears

- Playing golf

- Counting your eye floaters

So you simply have to keep track and write down all the "exercise" you complete daily. Walked up the stairs—there's seventy calories burned. Opened a door—two calories burned. Closed the door—two more calories bite the dust. When I counted all these little activities, I found I was up to about seventeen minutes of exercise a day. Not bad. As a matter of fact, I'm ready for another workout. I think I'll go button my shirt.

Jack LaLanne

One guy who wouldn't be satisfied with just doing wimpy exercises like gardening is my favorite male exercise guru of all time, and the number-one example in this country for guys searching for the Fountain of Youth, Jack LaLanne. Jack was born during the early 1800s, I believe, and has been leading people to exercise ever since. Real exercise, not some fake, lame, celebrity exercises. Exercise that will get you in shape.

At the time this book went to press, LaLanne was a robust ninety-two-year-old who was still making the rounds of cable news shows along with his wife, Elaine. He's in better shape at ninety-two than I was at eighteen. Muscles still bulge from his torso; they just ripple a little lower than in years past. LaLanne is proof positive that exercise helps one achieve a healthy, active, longer life.

I remember when I was a kid watching LaLanne run around like a crazy man on TV, shouting at the home viewer to keep up with his exercises. LaLanne was sort of like Richard Simmons, only in long pants. Simmons is sort of a "you love him or you hate him" type. When I worked at *The Tonight Show* on days he guested, the staff kept a large bottle of aspirin around to deal with what was called a "Richard Simmons headache."

I never thought Richard was so bad. But he was no Jack LaLanne. LaLanne was a human cannonball. And the fact that he's still doing his thing in his nineties should be an inspiration to us all.

The Longevity Test

The purpose of this test is to allow people to calculate their life expectancy.

1. Your exercise habits . . .
    a. Vary greatly depending on your schedule.
    b. Could be better.
    c. Consist entirely of trying to get your pants over that enormous, bulbous, lardlike tissue that used to be your hips.
    (If c, subtract five years.)

2. You wear a seat belt . . .
    a. Rarely.
    b. Usually.
    c. Always. You're so frazzled from watching the evening news that you buckle up even when you're sitting in your La-Z-Boy at home.
    (If c, add one year.)

3. You get . . .
    a. Eight hours of sleep per night.
    b. Less than eight hours of sleep.
    c. Six to seven at night, but since you're a federal em-

ployee, you get another eight hours of sleep per day at the office.

(If c, add two years.)

4. Your celebrity fitness role model is . . .
   a. Bob's Big Boy.
   b. Dick Cheney.
   c. Jerrod from the Subway ads.
   d. The stars of *Celebrity Fit Club.*
   (Any of the above, subtract three years.)

5. Studies have shown that pets lower their owners' blood pressure. Your pet's name is . . .
   a. Rover.
   b. Daisy.
   c. Killer, the Psycho Man-Eating Pit Bull.
   d. Montecore the Tiger (who attacked Roy, of Siegfried and Roy).
   e. None of the above.
   (If c or d, subtract six years.)

6. Your eating habits are . . .
   a. Good.
   b. Fair.
   c. Uncertain. You're having trouble reading this, as the longevity test is covered with fudge.
   d. Unfaltering. Once, as you were choking, you ate a

meatball sandwich while your wife performed the Heimlich maneuver.

(If c or d, subtract two years.)

7. Your favorite form of recreation is . . .

    a. Golf.

    b. Tennis.

    c. Pie-eating.

    (If c, subtract eight years. If a, subtract nine years.)

8. When it comes to social interaction you . . .

    a. Have many friends.

    b. Have several close friends.

    c. Make the Unabomber look like Oprah.

    (If c, subtract five years.)

9. The celebrity people say you most resemble is . . .

    a. Fred Flintstone.

    b. Jude Law.

    c. The guy in the "before" picture in Slim-Fast ads.

    d. One of the Teletubbies.

    e. Abe Vigoda, only older.

    (If a, c, d, or e, subtract three years.)

10. How would you rate your stress level?

    a. I have little stress.

    b. I developed a duodenal ulcer worrying about whether Brad and Jen will get back together.

    c. I get panic attacks when bread pops out of the toaster.

(If b *or* c, *subtract seven years.)*

11. How often do you see a doctor?

    a. Annually.

    b. I play golf on Wednesdays, so I see dozens of doctors every week.

    c. I'm a woman, so I see a doctor if I get a paper cut or a hangnail or I'm feeling blue.

    d. I'm a guy, so I have regular checkups every thirty-five years.

(If d, *subtract two years.)*

12. If you answered *d* to the above question, why don't you see your doctor more often?

    a. Duh—I'm a guy.

    b. Two words: rubber gloves.

    c. I have an HMO, so to make an appointment, I have to wait till my primary care physician gets off work at the Coffee Bean.

(If c, *subtract one year.)*

Key: If you took the time to answer these dumb questions, you lead a relaxed, non–Type A life and should live to be one hundred.

What Have We Learned?

The bottom line is that men are taking more of an interest in their health and in staying young than we have in the past, but we still have a ways to go. We're certainly aided by new advances. LASIK eye surgery has made it possible for us to toss away our glasses. Despite the fact that my uncorrected vision is so bad that they test my vision by planting me in the center of the examination room and asking me to point to the door (outside a drive-through restaurant, I once spent five minutes talking to a clown's head I thought I went to high school with), I haven't had LASIK yet because it's still too new, in my book. Of course, that's the same reason I shy away from flu shots and penicillin. Still in the experimental stages.

We continue to be simultaneously bemused/intrigued/repulsed by new studies regarding longevity. Case in point: A recent study claims that ultra-low-calorie diets are the key to a long life. Such a diet isn't for the masses. Most of us feel that life without doughnuts and cake is not a life worth living.

Guys shy away from medical advances and studies we don't completely understand. And we have a health-care system in this country that makes the DMV look like a well-oiled machine. But if a guy takes care of himself, he might just be able to diminish his exposure to that system.

Men are competitive by nature. Even if we're not particularly vain, just hearing that Fred Jones down the street looks "ten years younger and can run a mile in eight minutes" may be enough to get us out of our hammocks. We want to look eleven years younger and be able to run a mile in less than eight minutes.

So compete with your friends and neighbors. It's the American way. If your coworker's cholesterol is 180, try to get yours down to 160.

Humiliating your neighbor isn't the only incentive for taking care of yourself though. Surveys show that healthy-looking people who stay in shape tend to advance in the workplace and get the best jobs and promotions. This can be a motivating tool for men. Not only that, but taking care of yourself can save you a small fortune in medical bills over your lifetime. Men may claim the reason they don't practice good health habits is that they're not afraid of dying, but the cost of medical care is a whole new fear factor.

On the positive side, breakthroughs and new developments keep emerging to help us look and feel better.

I probably should tell you that what matters is what's on the inside, and if you think positively about yourself, you'll feel good and live longer. But men don't think like that. We want shortcuts. So until Doc Bob comes on Channel 6 and tells us about a new

What Have We Learned?

Fountain of Youth pill that we can take in the morning (with food—preferably bacon and fried eggs) that will help us live longer and feel great, we're willing to do only so much.

Fortunately, we don't need to do much. I think I have this aging problem solved. The United States is one of the few countries in the world that puts a premium on youth. In many places, the Far East, for example, the elderly run the show and are revered. So in lieu of searching for the Fountain of Youth, we can look into time-shares in Shanghai.

And the Winner Is . . .

So who came closest to finding the legendary Fountain of Youth? The men? The women? Both?

The answer, I'm afraid, is neither. No matter how much so many want it to be true, the Fountain of Youth does not exist. Someone probably dreamed it up one day after looking at his or her latest driver's license picture. Surely, there must be a Fountain of Youth—some magical pool of water that would reverse the effects of time. But as that person and every searcher since has discovered, the Fountain of Youth is merely a fantasy. You can search for it with MapQuest, but it won't show up. Not the real one, anyway. Only Ponce de León's Florida natural spring.

Like it or not, the truth is simply this: youth was never intended to be our permanent state. We were created to mature, to take life as it comes—the good and the bad, summer after summer, winter after winter—and then to pass on to others what we've learned from those experiences. That's the secret to eternal youth. It's not found in any spring of magic water. It's found in contentment, personal growth, deep faith, and inner joy. Those are the qualities that keep us young. Ponce de León was searching for something he could have found inside himself all along, without ever setting sail.

Then again, he was in his fifties, and it was a cruise to Florida. So who can blame him?

About the Authors

Martha Bolton is the author of more than seventy books of humor, including the "Official" Book series. She was a staff writer for Bob Hope for more than fifteen years and has been nominated for an Emmy and a Dove Award. She is the recipient of four Angel Awards. She has also written for Phyllis Diller, Wayne Newton's USO shows, and numerous others.

Brad Dickson was a monologue staff writer for *The Tonight Show with Jay Leno* for fourteen years. Before that he was a working screenwriter, placing several screenplays with motion picture companies. Since leaving *The Tonight Show,* he has been writing recurring humor columns for the *Los Angeles Times, L.A. Daily News,* and the *Jewish World Review* website. He has also developed a groundbreaking pilot for a major television network. He and Martha coauthored *Maybe Life's Just Not That Into You.*